NORTH
DUBLIN

City and Environs

NORTH DUBLIN

DUBLIN

City and Environs

———◆✦◆———

Dillon Cosgrave

NONSUCH

First published 1909
Copyright © in this edition 2005
Nonsuch Publishing
73 Lower Leeson Street,
Dublin 2
Ireland

www.nonsuchireland.com

© Dillon Cosgrave 2005

A catalogue record for this book is available from the National Library.

ISBN 1 84588 533 3

Typesetting and origination by Nonsuch Publishing Limited
Printed in Great Britain

Contents

INTRODUCTION

D UBLIN IS A CITY MANY times written of, whether in poetry, prose or song, but by the end of the nineteenth century and the start of the twentieth there was a distinct feeling that the changes and character of North Dublin had not been included in those writings.

Dillon Cosgrave set about his task of writing a history of the Northern portion of Dublin city and county because, as he states in his original preface, 'that district has hitherto been somewhat neglected.' The nature of Dublin, its division into a North Side and a South Side populated by two distinct and diverse tribes, featuring two cultures and two modes of thinking, made this situation undesirable. Not just to the proud Northsiders but also to the Southsiders who desired to read of a city they knew little of and probably experienced less.

The charge of writing the history of even a part of a city as old as Dublin is complex and confusing but that very difficulty is managed very comprehensively by Cosgrave. This book is a faithful reproduction of his work first published in 1909 and reissued in 1931 in an updated edition.

Cosgrave populates his work with references to those who lived still on the streets he refers to and also to the names of bygone days still well remembered. To the modern reader, the names of Lords, Ladies, Earls and

Viscounts reflects the passing of a very different Dublin, indeed a very different Ireland. The names of previously well known artists and academics, like Charles Lever, the oft forgotten popular Irish writer of the nineteenth century, litter the text too, as Cosgrave gives life to the streets through the stories of those who lived and worked on them and wrote of them.

Perhaps the most thrilling aspect of this book though is the portrait that Cosgrave successfully paints of the North Side of Dublin city and county. He portrays a story of growth through time; reclamations from the sea, the opening of parts of the northern slice of the county, the unsightly and often inconvenient encroachment of the railways and the development of Howth and the rest of the coastline.

Cosgrave's work stands the test of time in its picture of North Dublin. Although now outdated by developments and changes that even a decade ago we could not have imagined, *North Dublin City & Environs* presents still a recognizable picture of the northern half of Dublin city and county.

Dublin, October 2005.

Preface to the Original Edition

THERE SEEMS TO BE REASON to say something about the north side of the City of Dublin, as that district has hitherto been somewhat neglected. In Gilbert's otherwise excellent three-volume *History of the City of Dublin* it is altogether ignored.

The County was well done by John D'Alton many years ago, and has been well done once more by Mr F. Elrington Ball. Names have received special attention, as in them much interesting history is frequently embodied.

I desire to express my thanks to the Librarian and his assistants for their courtesy in facilitating my researches in the National Library.

D.C.

CHAPTER I

WEST OF CHURCH STREET

AND THE FINGLAS ROAD

U P TO THE END OF the seventeenth century the portion of the City of Dublin, lying to the north of the river Liffey, was very small.

It consisted mainly of Church Street, then the principal thoroughfare, and a few streets to the east and west of it: from the east side out to the sea was a stretch of open country in which lay the suppressed Abbey of St Mary, and the Dominican Priory nearer to the river[1]. The sea then came in much farther to the westward than it does now, the coast-line at that time running from Clontarf by Ballybough to where are now the North Strand Road and Amiens Street, and, turning round by what is now Beresford Place, it reached by Strand Street to the site of Essex Bridge.

Nothing to east of this line had yet been recovered from the sea. The tidal waters of the river flowed considerably north of the present line of quays, and on retiring left exposed at ebb a large slob land. Up to the last quarter of the seventeenth century there was only one bridge over the Liffey in Dublin, that is the bridge called Dublin Bridge or the Old Bridge, connecting Church Street with Bridge Street. On the older maps it is called emphatically The Bridge.

This was the only bridge existing because it was the only one needed. It was built by King John in 1210, and rebuilt by the Dominicans in 1385. They had their convent on the site of the Four Courts and received toll through one of their lay brothers from those who crossed the bridge. From the dissolution of the monasteries until 1582 the Inns of Court were on the site of this

Convent, from 1582 to 1695 the Courts, and the Inns of Court again until the end of the eighteenth century. The present Four Courts were completed by James Gandon in 1796 at a cost of £200,000[2]. During the construction of the present Whitworth Bridge here, traces were discovered of the foundations of the bridge before that of King John, constructed by the ancient Irish, or by the Scandinavians. In pursuing our exploration of North Dublin it will be convenient then to start from this very ancient thoroughfare, Church Street, and, having glanced at the city's westward progress, follow its growth eastward till it reaches the sea. We shall also travel along the principal roads running northward through the county as we meet them issuing from the great thoroughfares of the city.

Before beginning a detailed description of the streets it may be well to refer to the bridges that now span the river which forms the southern limit of the district we propose to describe, and must be our Rubicon. They number twelve, and, beginning with the most western, are in the order of their occurrence as follows:

In the county, Leixlip Bridge (southern half), the northern half being in the County of Kildare; Lucan Bridge and Chapelizod Bridge (southern half). Within the city boundary; Chapelizod Bridge (northern half), Sarah Bridge, built in 1791 on the site of Island Bridge. The King's Bridge, built in 1828. Victoria Bridge, built in 1863, occupies the site of the old wooden bridge called Bloody Bridge; the latter derived its sanguinary name from a fatal affray in 1671 the year after its erection, in which the partisans of a formerly existing ferry figured largely; it was rebuilt of stone in 1704 and named Barrack Bridge. The fine gate of the Royal Hospital was erected at Barrack Bridge by Francis Johnston in 1812, and removed to its present position in 1846. The Queen's Bridge, built in 1776 (the oldest existing Dublin bridge over the Liffey), preceded by Arran Bridge, built in 1683, appears as Bridewell Bridge, 1756, called after the Bridewell in Smithfield; and Ellis's Bridge, 1766. Whitworth Bridge built in 1818, occupies the site of the Old Bridge built by the ancient Irish or Scandinavians; afterwards, as stated above, by King John in 1210, and rebuilt by the Dominicans in 1385. Little John, standing on this bridge in 1189, is said to have discharged from his bow an arrow which reached a hillock on Oxmantown Green, a very long distance. Richmond Bridge, built in 1813, formerly Ormond Bridge, which was built in 1683 and swept away in 1806. Grattan Bridge, built in 1874, on the site of Essex Bridge, which was originally built in 1676, and rebuilt in 1755. Wellington, or The Metal, Bridge, built in 1816. O'Connell Bridge, built in 1880 on the site of Carlisle Bridge, which was erected in 1794. Butt Bridge, built in 1879, enlarged in 1932.

Starting from the ancient thoroughfare of Church Street, we pass on the west the old Church of St Michan, founded in 1095, from which the street derives its name. It is the oldest building on the north side of the city, and the oldest in Dublin, except one, Christ Church, which exceeds it in age by but a few years. It was rebuilt in the seventeenth century, but the tower may be as old as the eleventh century. Some portions of the edifice, too, date from the time of its original foundation. The vaults are celebrated for the antiseptic quality of the air, which has preserved bodies for centuries. This property has been ascribed by some writers to the dryness arising from the yellow limestone of the walls, but assigned by others to various causes. Henry and John Sheares, the United Irishmen, were buried here, and Charles Lucas, Oliver Bond and the Rev. William Jackson in the adjoining churchyard. The present fine Capuchin Church of St Mary of the Angels was erected in 1864. Earlier Capuchin churches had been erected here in 1720 and 1796.

To the west of this very old road at its Dublin extremity, lie Arbour Hill, famous for its memories of Robin Hood's gigantic lieutenant, humorously called Little John; and Montpelier Hill, which contained the residence of a Royal Duke about the year 1850. This was the late Duke of Cambridge, then Prince George of Cambridge, grandson of George III, and first cousin of Queen Victoria. He was in Dublin as an officer of the army and member of the Dublin garrison. He afterwards commanded the Dublin District, and a few years later served in the Crimea, and was Commander-in-Chief of the British Army for many years. He lived here for a very short time, his residence for the greater part of his stay in Dublin being at his quarters in the adjoining Royal Barracks. He was married to Miss Louisa Farebrother, an actress. As this marriage was contracted without the consent of the then sovereign, Queen Victoria, it was contrary to the Royal Marriage Act, passed in the reign, and at the wish, of George III, and was always regarded as morganatic. The eldest son, the late Colonel Fitzgeorge, did not succeed to the title of Duke of Cambridge. The Royal Barrack was built in the year of Blenheim, 1704. Here also are found Barrack Street, now Benburb Street, called by D'Alton 'the Suburra of Dublin', and the short street leading to Bloody Bridge, first called Cuffe Street, then Silver Street for a hundred years, and now. Ellis Street since 1872. Under the name of Silver Street it has been made known to thousands who have never seen Dublin, as the scene of the military street fight in *Belts*, one of the *Barrack-room Ballads*. There are also the King's Hospital, Oxmantown, a famous old Protestant School, founded in 1670 in what is now Queen Street. The present building was begun in 1773, and was never quite finished. Both the old and new Bluecoat Schools, as they are called, were built on what was formerly Oxmantown Green, of which the school field is the last surviving portion.[3] Oxmantown Green was once covered by a wood. In 1008 William Rufus had the roof of Westminster Hall constructed of Oxmantown timber. Dermot O'Hurley, Archbishop of Cashel, was martyred on Oxmantown Green on the 19th of June, 1584[4].

Oxmantown was once a village separate from Dublin. It occupied the district where now stand Church Street (southern end), Smithfield, Bow Street, Queen Street, Blackhall Street, Hendrick Street, the western half of North King Street, and, as said above, the King's Hospital. The name is derived from the Ostmen or Eastmen, a name given to the Scandinavians, who lived east of Ireland and England. The Scandinavians seem to have made Oxmantown their residence after the Norman Conquest. Nowadays we should consider Scandinavia the very near East. The name Oxman town recalls not only the heroic memory of Clontarf, but also those earlier days when Dublin was a Scandinavian kingdom whose kings had such Hibernicised names as Sitric MacAuliffe and Hasculph MacTorkill. The latter was King of Dublin[5] when the city surrendered to Strongbow and Milo de Cogan on the 21st of September, 1170. These Danish names have been appropriately commemorated lately by bestowing them on a number of new roads between Arbour Hill and the North Circular Road near old Oxmantown. The postal address, 'King's Hospital, Oxmantown', still preserves the name of this ancient district.

To the west of Church Street we also find the Haymarket; Smithfield, where the Earl of Bective, ancestor of the Marquess of Headfort, had his town residence in the eighteenth century; Queen Street and Thundercut Alley; and the splendid and spacious Blackhall Street, built in 1789, and named after Sir Thomas Blackhall who was Lord Mayor in 1769. Whitehall Street was near this a century ago. The name Queen Street, founded in 1687, and Queen's Bridge adjoining, are probably from Catharine of Braganza, consort of Charles II. Irwin's *Guide to Dublin*, published in 1853, speaking specially of Blackhall Street, says that this is the part of Dublin enjoying the most mild and genial climate, and that in gardens here the grape and the fig ripen in the open air. To the west of old Church Street lay also Gravel Walk, afterwards Tighe Street, now part of Benburb Street; Sand Quay, afterwards Pembroke Quay, now rebuilt and called Sarsfield Quay, Gravel Walk Slip, a dock on the riverside where Blackhall Place now meets the quay; and Arran Quay, called after the Earl of Arran, a younger son of the Duke of Ormonde, where Edmund Burke was born (at No 12)[6]. It was in the year 1750 that he went to London like many Irishmen 'to seek his fortune', which he found. No. 32 Arran Quay was the place of business of Charles Haliday, already referred to as the historian of the Scandinavian Kingdom of Dublin.

West of Arran Quay is Ellis's Quay, called after the family of Agar-Ellis, Viscounts Clifden, who had a valuable leasehold interest from the Corporation of Dublin extending from Arran Quay to the Phoenix Park. Some of the leases are dated 1662, and their maps show the Liffey as the southern boundary of the Ellis property. Lord Clifden resided on Arran Quay[7]. Parkgate Street[8] and Conyngham Road are names of the old thoroughfare from Dublin to Chapelizod and Lucan. Before the King's Bridge was built in 1828, there was a ferry at this part of Parkgate Street. Yet this circumstance scarcely justified an assertion made a few years since in the account of a famous Dublin trial of over a century ago in the pages of a Dublin magazine. The writer was puzzled by the statement in the old newspaper he was consulting that the criminal was believed to have left Dublin by the Parkgate packet. He explained it by asserting that the packet started from the Park Gate. But the Dublin cross-channel vessels corresponding to the present Holyhead service sailed in those days to Parkgate in Cheshire. There is a reference to this in the humorous old song of Billy O'Rourke:

> *I engaged with the captain for eight thirteens*
> *To carry me over to Parkgate.*
> *But before the ship went half the way,*
> *She went at a terribly hard gait.*

The cessation of the Dublin traffic was a great blow to Parkgate, which is now a kind of obsolete coast village.

Close by Old Church Street on the west were three streets worthy of some notice. The first was the Hangman's Lane, a name naturally not much relished by the inhabitants, and consequently corrupted into. Hammond Lane[9], which it is still called. Besides Hammond Lane there was Lough Buoy, the present Bow Street, but called up to the early part of the eighteenth century by the old Irish name from a large pond at the north, or King Street, end which was probably connected with the Channel Row branch of the Bradoge. There was also May Lane, perhaps so called from the surname May, but mentioned in the *Maybush*, an old ballad to be found in *Ireland a Hundred and Twenty years Ago*[10]. The butchers of Ormond Market had their Maybush in Smithfield.

Turning next from the junction of Church Street with North King Street or North Brunswick Street we follow the course of a road by Stonybatter even older than that which is continued from Church Street to Ashbourne or Naul. North King Street is found as 'King Street, Oxmantown,' in 1552, and is probably the same as King's Lane, Oxmantown, in 1438. King Street had at least two convents of the Poor Clares at different times in the eighteenth century, both on the north side of the street, the later near Blackhall Place and the earlier nearer to Church Street, the present No. 63 North King Street, formerly a Medical School and now a National School. In the latter a very old lady died in 1730 who had been famous in the world in her youth. This was Frances Jennings, sister of Sarah, Duchess of Marlborough, and widow of Richard Talbot, Earl and Duke of Tyrconnell, James II's Lord Lieutenant. He died in Limerick during the siege. The Poor Clares finally left North King Street in 1825, and returned to Galway, from which they had originally come. Redcow Lane, King Street, near their convent, seems to have taken its name from an inn sign. In the eighteenth century there were Augustinian nuns in Russell Court. This court was situated between the Capuchin Church and May Lane.

The parallel street to North King Street, viz., North Brunswick Street, obviously derives its name from Charles, Duke of Brunswick, who married in 1764 Princess Augusta, sister of George III. He was killed at Jena in 1806, and his son and successor at Les Quatre Bras, 16th June, 1815. It was called before 1766 Channel Row, and derived its old name, still sometimes heard, from a channel connected with the little stream called the Bradoge. This little brook (which has a namesake at Bundoran) also gave its name to Bradoge Lane, now the southern portion of Halston Street, under which it flows. We shall meet this little river again later on.

Having crossed the Bradoge and passed Richmond Hospital, where once stood 'Channel Row Nunnery', the predecessor of Cabra Convent, we reach Stonybatter, a name recalling still more ancient times. The last part of the word is the Irish *bothar*, a road; and this very road was called Bothar-na-gcloch, road of the stones. It is likely that this street formed part of the old road from Tara by the sea to Wicklow, made in the second century and crossing the Liffey at the ford of hurdles (Ath Cliath) where Whitworth Bridge now stands. As is well-known Dublin derives its old Irish name, *Baile Atha Cliath*, from this ancient ford. If the name Stonybatter is really seventeen hundred years old, it must surely be granted the palm for antiquity amongst Dublin street-names. The northern end of Stonybatter received its present name of Manor Street in 1780 from the Manor of Grangegorman in which it was situated. The Manor House is now the police barrack in that street. The owner of the Manor in the reign of Charles II was Sir Thomas Stanley, from whom the short Street called Stanley Street, off North Brunswick Street, is named. His daughter Sarah married in 1663 Henry Monck, grandfather of the first Lord Monck. To this family the estate passed, and their long association with the district is commemorated in such names as Monck Place, Royse Road, from the name of a family intermarried with the Moncks, Rathdown Road and Terrace, from the title of Earl of Rathdowne, enjoyed by one of the Viscounts Monck, and Charleville Road and Terrace and Enniskerry Road, from the name of their residence near Enniskerry, Co. Wicklow.

The apex of a triangle formed by the two streets at the north end of Manor Street marks the site of a village before Dublin had extended so far.[11] The western or left hand side of the Oxmantown triangle was called Blackhorse Lane from this point to Castleknock until 1780, when the portion from Manor Street (so named in the same year) to the Circular Road, was given the name of Aughrim Street, as a memorial of the Battle of Aughrim, fought on the 12th of July, 1691. Such a memorial is characteristic of the sway of Orangeism in municipal affairs in the days of the old Corporation, whose civic patriotism was not so liberal as to include consideration for the Catholic majority of Ireland and of Dublin. The fine Parish Church of the Holy Family in this street was built in 1880. The present Blackhorse Lane, starting from the Dublin Corporation Abattoir (the Ordnance map misspelled Abbatoir), derives its name from the Black Horse tavern, better known to Dubliners as 'Nancy Hand's' from its popular hostess at the time, or the 'Hole in the Wall', from a turn stile into the adjoining Phoenix Park. Blackhorse Lane passes an old well called the Poor Man's Well, and, nearer to Dublin, the Military Cemetery and Marlborough Cavalry Barrack, built when Lord Wolseley was Commander-in-Chief. About the same time he produced his *Life of Marlborough*[12]. Marlborough Road is named from it

Prussia Street received its name in 1765 from Frederick the Great, King of Prussia. Frederick, who belonged to the Hohenzollern family, Electors of Brandenburg, was then one of the most prominent personages in Europe. The tall old house in Prussia Street, now the City Arms Hotel, was formerly the residence of one of the Jameson family, the well-known distillers, who came to Dublin from Scotland. At an earlier period it was inhabited by Henry Stevens Reily from whom is named the bridge over the Royal Canal on the Ratoath Road, a continuation of Prussia Street. He is the 'Squire O'Reilly' of Burton's strange topographical romance of Oxman town.

Before 1765 Prussia Street and its continuation were called Cabragh Lane; as the continuation is still called Old Cabra Road in contradistinction to the new Cabra Road, starting from St Peter's Church and joining the old road at the gate of the Deaf and Dumb Institution, the point of inter section of the roads to Navan and Ratoath. The little building which preceded the present fine Church was erected in 1823, and, after fifteen years, handed over to the Congregation of the Mission on its establishment in Ireland. The Old Cabra Road is connected with Blackhorse Lane by a thoroughfare oddly called Blind Lane, for it is not a blind lane or cul-de-sac, but a complete thoroughfare. Old Cabra Road passes on the right Cabra House, once the residence of Lord Norbury, John Toler, who shot ahead in life by means of duelling pistols, and, when he had shot his way to the bench, became the terror of prisoners in Ireland over a century ago. He was more famous for wit than for feeling. On the left is Cabra Convent, founded in 1819 in the old mansion of the Arthurs. Except for a brief stay in Clontarf, in a house still called Convent House in the Green Lanes, the Dominican nuns had inhabited 'Channel Row Nunnery' for nearly a hundred years. The last- named Convent had been built originally for Benedictine nuns in the reign of James II.

Where the road crosses Reilly's Bridge on the Canal, named after Henry Stevens Reily, one of the original Directors of the Royal Canal Company, a fine view is obtained of the picturesque ruin of Finglaswood House, within living memory the residence of a family named Savage. The country lane adjoining is still called Savage's Lane and leads past the secluded residence of St. Helena, by the Long Walk, to the village of Finglas. Old Cabra Road descends into the valley of the River Tolka at the village of Cardiff's Bridge. Some distance to the left, at Pelletstown, there was a castle in ruins some years ago, of which not a vestige remains. Pelletstown House adjoining was once the residence of a young officer, Sir John French, who was afterwards Field Marshal the Earl of Ypres. On a road north of this is the Royal Observatory at Dunsink. From Cardiff's Bridge the main road, passing not far from a place with the familiar name of Killester, leads into the little town of Ratoath in the County of Meath.

Following out Church Street to its northern extremity, we reach Constitution Hill[13], formerly North Townsend Street, and in earlier times known, with the adjoining district, by the Irish name of Glasmanoge. The Irish Parliament met here once on the occasion of a plague in the city. We pass next under what was, until a short time ago, the Foster Aqueduct, called after the last Speaker of the Irish House of Commons. This aqueduct conducted the water of the Royal Canal to a basin in the Terminus which was filled up about fifty years ago. Some of the hotels in this neighbourhood are older than the railway, having been established for the accommodation of passengers on the Canal. This service, of which a good description is to be found in Lever's *Tom Burke* and *Jack Hinton*, was at one time very popular.

The Royal Canal was purchased about the year 1850 by the Midland Great Western Railway Company, an event which has gradually led to the almost total abandonment of the Canal. A map of the end of the eighteenth century marks as 'Overfal' another branch of the Royal Canal, apparently never made, opening northward opposite the City Branch. Blaquiere Bridge, on the North Circular Road, spanning the City Branch of the Canal, now filled up, took its name from Sir John (Lord) de Blaquiere, a Director of the Company. On the City Branch Canal Bank, behind a house on Phibsborough Road, is found the inscription Cumnor Hall, from the house in which Amy Robsart, the wife of Elizabeth's favourite Dudley, afterwards Earl of Leicester, is said to have been murdered in 1560 by her husband's orders. The house by the Canal was probably named by some admirer of Scott's *Kenilworth* into which the tragic story is introduced. Phibsborough Road., the thoroughfare from the Aqueduct to Westmoreland Bridge, as well as Phibsborough Avenue and Phibsborough, popularly called 'the Borough', are called in older documents

Phipps borough, and are named from the family of Phibbs or Phipps long connected with the County of Sligo.

There are a few interesting names to be mentioned on the North Circular Road between Phibsborough and the Park. St. Dymphna's, the residence of the Medical Superintendent of the Grangegorman Mental Asylum, is called after that Irish virgin, martyred in Belgium, whose feast occurs on the 15th of May. She has always been regarded in Belgium as the protectress of the insane, and there is a great Asylum dedicated to her at Gheel in that country. Cumberland Place, of which the name-plate bears date 1851, is called after Ernest, Duke of Cumberland and King of Hanover, a son of George III, who died in that year. As he was a member of the Orange Society, we may assume that this terrace was named by, some extreme Conservative. Lorne Terrace is from the Marquess of Lorne, afterwards Duke of Argyle, brother-in-law of Edward VII. Prince Patrick Terrace is from Edward VII's military brother, Prince Patrick, now the Duke of Connaught. Bessborough Terrace, like Bessborough Avenue, North Strand, is from the Irish peer who died Lord Lieutenant in 1847, and the last terrace, Wodehouse Terrace, is from Lord Wodehouse, afterwards Earl of Kimberley, who was Lord Lieutenant 1864-6, in the exciting Fenian times. Sullivan Street, close by, is called after T.D. Sullivan who was Lord Mayor in 1886 and 1887, and Aberdeen Street from a former Viceroy.

The district of Grangegorman, comprising five townlands of that name and lying between Phibsborough Road and the Phoenix Park, includes some places and names worthy of notice. Grangegorman and Glasnevin belonged at a period long before the Norman Invasion to the Augustinian Priory of the Holy Trinity, the predecessor of Christ Church. The name of Stanhope Street dates from 1792, a long time after the Vice-royalty, 1745-7, of the famous Philip Dormer Stanhope, Earl of Chester field, or of that of his kinsman and immediate successor in the Viceroyalty, William Stanhope, first Earl of Harrington. Kirwan Street, joining Grangegorman Lane to Manor Street, is called after Dr. James Kirwan, Coroner of Dublin, and a member of one of the Tribes of Galway, a former owner of property here. There was a great wood called Sallcock's Wood where Quarry Lane and the Cabra Road now intersect. Here the O'Tooles, returning from a successful foray in Fingal, defeated the citizens of Dublin who tried to intercept them.

CHAPTER II

THE PHOENIX PARK AND

THE BARONY OF THE TYRRELS (CASTLEKNOCK)

THE PHOENIX PARK, ONE OF the chief beauties of Dublin north of the Liffey, is 1,752 acres 3 roods and 21 perches in extent, and about seven miles in circumference. The Park was the scene of the Eucharistic Congress in 1932. It originally included not only the Conyngham Road and the land between that and the river but also the large tract to the south of the Liffey which had belonged to the Royal Hospital since its erection in 1684. Some additional land farther west, also south of the river and the Conyngham Road, has recently been acquired for the Park. The Park, as we know it, has been confined within the present wall since 1671. The wall was made for the sake of the deer which were here even then. The date shows that the Park, like the Royal Hospital and St. Stephen's Green, was practically begun in the reign of Charles II., one of the most flourishing periods in the history of the development of the city of Dublin, The man to whom we owe the Park and the other improvements of that epoch, was James Butler, the celebrated first Duke of Ormonde, who spent his long life in the faithful service of the two Charleses, father and son. His ideas on the development of the city of Dublin were most liberal and magnificent.

The nucleus of the Park, as designed by Ormonde, was formed by the lands of the Knights Hospitallers of Kilmainham, which had reverted to the Crown on the dissolution of the monasteries by Henry VIII. This was reinforced by extensive purchases of land to the north and west of the monastic lands.

The name of the Phoenix Park arises, as is well known, from a misconception. The real name is Fionn Uisge or clear water, the Irish name for a chalybeate spa in the Park which was once quite famous. When in the height of its fame the Duchess of Richmond enclosed it in a small building of Portland stone. There seems to be a strange misunderstanding as to the situation of this spa. While a modern authority asserts that it is near the Phoenix Column, D'Alton describes it as 'contiguous to' the Zoological Gardens. From his detailed and minute description the reader comes to the conclusion that the 'shady glen' which he describes as its locality, must have been the spot between the Viceregal and the Zoological Garden Ponds where there is still a spring, although it is now covered over. This would seem to be established by the following passage 'Adjacent to the spa is a building, formerly used as an engine- house for, supplying the Military Infirmary with water, that necessity having however ceased, the edifice is converted into a ranger's lodge.' This building is obviously the picturesque cottage of the Park Constable, with the overhanging roof; at the northern extremity of the Zoological Gardens. D'Alton can hardly have been mistaken as to the situation of the spa of Fionn Uisge, as, when he wrote, it still enjoyed some vogue.

Warburton, Whitelaw and Walsh who wrote *The History of the City of Dublin* twenty years before D'Alton's book appeared, and Wakeman, who wrote in recent years, concur in stating that the Fionn Uisge was situated at the end of the present Zoological Gardens. The late Caesar Litton Falkiner accepted the Irish etymology, but thought very reasonably that the Fionn Uisge should have been near the Phoenix House, that is in the neighbourhood of the present Magazine Fort. D'Alton refers to 'the old Manor-house of Fionnuiske', but places the Fionn Uisge spring at the end of the Zoological Gardens.

The mistake in the name of the Park is of old date. Early in the seventeenth century (1619) we hear of the Manor House of the Phoenix, which stood on the top of Thomas's Hill, where the Magazine Fort stands now. Mr. Elrington Ball thinks the Phoenix House was perhaps called so as a phoenix of houses from its commanding position and splendid• outlook (*History of the County of Dublin*, Part IV, page 180). This house became the summer residence of the Viceroys in the reign of James I, and continued to be so used until it was superseded towards the end of the same century by a house in Chapelizod. Henry Cromwell resided in the Phoenix House for some time. It is also recorded that in 1671 'the Phoenix and Newtown lands', formerly in the possession of Christopher Fagan of Feltrim and Alderman Daniel Hutchinson, were purchased on the royal mandate for £3,000 by the Duke of Ormonde in trust for Charles II. The new Park is referred to as 'the Phoenix Park' in a record of 1675, and again in 1741. In 1711 during Queen Anne's reign, it is described as 'the Queen's garden at the Phoenix'.

It was not, however, until the 29th of March, 1747, that the mistake as to the origin of the name was perpetuated by the erection, during the Earl of Chesterfield's Viceroyalty, of the well-known Phoenix Column on the Main Road between the present Viceregal and Chief Secretary's Lodges. Lord Chesterfield, who loved the classics, utilized the legend of the wonderful bird, whose name is supposed to have been derived from its bright colour, resembling the scarlet Phoenician dye. The fabulous Phoenix was an Arabian bird, but used to appear in Egypt. The classical fable went on to say that there was only one phoenix in the world at a time, that it lived five hundred years and then burned itself to death, and that a new phoenix for the succeeding period sprang from its ashes. The new phoenix rising from the flames surmounts Lord Chesterfield's fluted Corinthian column, which is thirty feet high and bears inscriptions stating that Lord Chesterfield erected the column and beautified the Park for the delight of the citizens. On the left side of the column viewed from the front there is a coat of arms with the motto *Exitus acta probat*, which may be translated; The event tests what has been done. The Phoenix was once surrounded by a large circle called the Ring. Many uneducated citizens of Dublin call the Phoenix the 'Eagle Monument', and the mistake is very natural. The presence of flames seems to be the principal distinction between the phoenix and the eagle as represented by sculptors.

Notwithstanding Lord Chesterfield's obscuration of this old Irish name the Park in general was greatly indebted to him. He planted the magnificent avenue of elms which suffered such havoc from the great storm on the night of the 26th of February, 1903. He planted many of the other woods and clumps of trees in the Park, and 'had it adorned', as the inscription on the Column says, in many ways. But above all it was he who conferred the lasting benefit of throwing open this splendid Park to the citizens of Dublin and the public in general[14].

The Park is entered by eight large gates, those of the City, the Circular Road, Cabra, Ashtown, Castleknock, Knockmaroon, Chapelizod and Island Bridge. There are also the gate at White's Avenue and turnstiles at Blackhorse

Lane, Chapelizod and Island Bridge. There are some private entrances in the western portion, remote from the city, as Farmleigh and Mount Sackville Convent. There is also an entrance from the Marlborough Cavalry Barrack.

There are still over one thousand acres of the Park open to the public. The remainder of its area is occupied by various Government establishments. The most considerable of these is the Viceregal Lodge. This was built in 1751 for the private residence of Nathaniel Clements, chief ranger of the Park in the middle of the eighteenth century. Charles Gardiner, father of the first Lord Mountjoy, and Lord George Sackville held minor rangerships about the same time. The house was purchased from Clements's son, Robert, afterwards first Earl of Leitrim, in 1782, as a residence for the Viceroys. The Earl of Hardwicke added the wings in 1802, the Duke of Richmond the north portico and gate lodges in 1808, and Earl Whitworth the north front. It has been used as a residence by George IV, Victoria, Edward VII and George V during their visits to Ireland. The grounds are spacious and beautiful, and include the Private Secretary's Lodge. The western part of the grounds is called The Wilderness. The Chief Secretary's Lodge, now the residence' of the Envoy of the United States, was built by Sir John (Lord) de Blaquiere, a self-seeking placeman, who, for his self-imposed well-paid duties here, was nicknamed 'the King's Cowboy', and has also fine and extensive grounds adjoining it; and the Under Secretary's, formerly Ashtown Castle, to the north of the Main Road, must be mentioned in an account of the Phoenix Park as the residence of the famous Thomas Drummond who suppressed a considerable Park nuisance of his time, the Sunday drinking booths. It is now the residence of the Nuncio Apostolic, Most Rev. Paschal Robinson, Archbishop of Tyana.

Other enclosed portions of the Park are: Mount joy Barrack, built by Luke Gardiner, Park ranger, and inhibited by him and by his son and grandson, Charles Gardiner. and Luke, first Lord Mountjoy; afterwards a cavalry and an infantry barrack, and now the head-quarters' of the Ordnance Survey of Ireland; the beautiful Gardens of the Royal Zoological Society, now greatly improved and deservedly most popular (it should be remembered that they keep their centenary this year) ; the Royal Hibernian Military School, founded in 1769; the, Military Infirmary adjoining the People's Garden; the Magazine Fort, begun by the Earl of Wharton, and the subject of a well-known epigram by Swift; the Depot and Barrack of the Civic Guard; the Bailiff's Lodge near the Park Race course, various smaller cottages for the deerkeepers and gardeners, and three Park Constables' cottages, one already mentioned adjoining the Zoological Gardens, another near Mountjoy Barrack, and a third on the little hill of Knockmary, overhanging Chapelizod. Beside the last is a cromlech, which was dug up at this spot in 1838 and set up here[15]. Besides these enclosures there are large parts of the level and open portions of the Park near Dublin allotted to polo, cricket, football and hurling. The control of the Phoenix Park is vested in the Board of Public Works.

Towards the close of the eighteenth century, and about the time of the purchase of the Viceregal Lodge for the Lord Lieutenant, most of the Park rangerships were discontinued, and the residences of the rangers assigned to the chief officials of the Government. This step was taken at the instance of William Eden, afterwards Lord Auckland, Chief Secretary. Sir John de Blaquiere's house became the Chief Secretary's Lodge, Ashtown Castle the Under Secretary's, and Lord Mountjoy's house a barrack. The Under Secretary continued to be Ranger of the Phoenix Park until 1840, when this office was abolished on the death of Thomas Drummond, the last who held both offices.

The extensive plain called the Fifteen Acres, a complete misnomer, has always been appropriated to reviews and military exercises. It was formerly the duelling ground of Dublin. There were military camps in the Park in 1788 and 1797. The space between the Hibernian School and Chapelizod is marked Camp Ground on maps. At one time a conspicuous little hill, on which some old thorn trees grew, adjoining a small pond, was situated in the middle of this open plain of the Fifteen Acres. It was once an Artillery Butt. It was removed, no doubt on account of its inconvenience during reviews and manoeuvres. The plain called The White Fields is near Ashtown Gate. The smaller plain of the Nine Acres, with the slope called Trooper's Hill, lies north of the Main Road, next to the Zoological Gardens. The ground now occupied by the Phoenix Cricket Club, still marked Star Fort on the Ordnance Survey Maps, appears on older maps as covered by a veritable star-shaped fort.

The obelisk in honour of Wellington, constructed on the site of the Salute Battery, is 205 feet high and built of granite. Each of its four sides bears inscribed the names of his victories in India, France, Spain and Portugal respectively. His last and greatest battle in Belgium is reserved for a lower portion of the monument. It had been originally proposed to remove the statue of George II from the centre of St. Stephen's Green, and erect the Wellington Monument there, but the Corporation refused the site, holding that a King should not make way for a subject. There are two other monuments in the Park, the fine equestrian statue of Lord Gough, erected in 1880, and that of the seventh Earl of Carlisle in the People's Garden, to whose influence during his last Viceroyalty the creation of the People's Garden is due.

The roads of the Park are well known to Dublin pedestrians, equestrians, drivers, motorists and cyclists. The finest as a road is the splendid main road from Dublin to Castleknock, which was laid out by Lord Chesterfield, and was known for a long period to the citizens of Dublin by its appropriate name of Chesterfield Road. A different attraction, however, attaches to the winding road which begins at the Gough statue. Overhanging the Chapelizod public road, it passes the Fort and the Hibernian School, and leads to the Furry Glen, the prettiest portion of the Park. This road affords a splendid prospect of the valley of the Liffey, the plain beyond and the Dublin Mountains. The corresponding north road behind the Viceregal Lodge is of a more retired character. Seclusion is to be found in the roads to the far west of the Park, near Mountjoy Barracks. The road leading from the Phoenix to Chapelizod across the Fifteen Acres resembles some of the roads on the Curragh of Kildare; and the other road leading from the same point to Island Bridge is very pretty, traversing the valley of a little stream which it crosses at the White Bridge. This bridge gives name to the hill north of the Fort.

The Park is adorned by several sheets of water. There is a small pond in the Viceregal Grounds and also the fine pond, known to skaters, one of the largest in the county of Dublin. This is separated only by a road and a narrow space from the splendid pond which forms one of the greatest attractions of the beautiful Zoological Gardens. To the south of the road between these two miniature lakes and within the boundaries of the Zoological Gardens is the spa well, now covered, which is undoubtedly the original Fionn Uisge of D'Alton from which the Park is properly named, although there is a widely diffused opinion nowadays, supported by the authority of at least one popular writer on Dublin topography, that the famous chalybeate spring is situated near the Phoenix Column[16]. Other ponds are the Citadel Pond, between the Phoenix and Civil Service Cricket Grounds, with some smaller ponds not far off; the pretty ornamental pond of the People's Garden; Quarry Lake, with its island, near Mountjoy Barrack; and, last and most beautiful, the pond of the Furry Glen. Connected with the Furry Glen rivulet is Baker's Well near Knockmaroon Gate.

The principal woods in the portion of the Park open to the public are Bishop's Wood, now a part of the People's Garden; the Black Wood, of thorn trees, south of the Main Road; Pump Wood, near the last named thorn-wood; the Ash Wood and Butcher's Wood to the north and south respectively of Castleknock Gate, near which is a plain called the Stretch, and Oldtown Wood between the Chief Secretary's Lodge and Mountjoy Barrack. Another thickly-wooded spot is Half-Mile Hollow between the Fifteen Acres and the Park wall.

Leaving the Park by Ashtown Gate, the Royal Canal is reached in a very short time, at the point where it adjoins Ashtown House. The names of the Royal Canal bridges in this western part of the county - Longford, Ranelagh, Talbot, Granard, Kirkpatrick, Kennan, Callaghan, Pakenham and Collins's Bridges - are in most cases from those of original Directors of the Royal Canal Company, the Earl of Longford, Lord Ranelagh, the Earl of Granard, Alexander Kirkpatrick, The Hon. Thomas Pakenham, and John Collins. Longford Bridge is at Ashtown, Talbot Bridge on the high road to Navan and Enniskillen, Callaghan Bridge, formerly Carhampton Bridge, is at Clonsilla Railway Station, and Collins's Bridge at Lucan Station. The 'Deep Sinking', where the Canal is made between very high banks, is near Clonsilla and was once the scene of a disaster, when a passenger boat went down and many emigrants from Longford perished. The parish and village of Blanchardstown, on the Canal, are dedicated to St. Brigid.

Not far from Mulhuddart, a village beyond Blanchardstown are Hollywoodrath and Cruiserath, both called after old Norman families. Porterstown between Clonsilla and the Liffey, where there is a Catholic Church, was the birth place of Dr. Troy, Archbishop of Dublin. The Strawberry Beds are a series of lofty banks over hanging the Liffey Valley. Owing to their southerly aspect they have been long successfully used for the cultivation of strawberries. They have been for many years a favourite resort of the citizens of Dublin. On this bank is a townland with the odd name of Astagob. At the south-west angle of Luttrellstown, on the river, is a mill, the successor of the Devil's Mill, which was built by him according to the humorous account in Samuel Lover's *Stories of Ireland*. But D'Alton says the devil long prevented the building of a mill here; since one was built, however, 'the demon is now considered barred by a long interval of acquiescence', he tells us in his grand Johnsonian way[17].

A road off the main Road of the Phoenix Park leads to a gate of the Park and a quiet road called White's Avenue. This avenue runs between a house with the classic name of Mount Hybla (Leigh Hunt wrote a poem, *A Jar of Honey from Mount Hybla*) on the right, and Lord Iveagh's fine demesne of Farmleigh on the left. The tower at Farmleigh, where there is a clock which chimes the quarters, is a conspicuous object across the Phoenix Park and for miles around. White's Avenue terminates at the fate of St. Vincent's College, founded by the Vincentian Fathers in 1835, and still in a most flourishing condition. Castleknock College numbers amongst its past pupils several very eminent names in Church and State. The old castle here was the property of Hugh Tyrrell, one of the most powerful barons of the Pale. The Tyrrells long exercised almost regal sway over this western portion of the County of Dublin.

All this part of the valley of the Liffey is most beautiful, abounding in woodland and river scenery of the finest description. Its central point is Lucan which is, however, beyond the scope of this work as it lies for the most part south of the Liffey. The famous Patrick Sarsfleld, who came of an old Dublin family, was connected with this district as an owner of property, and by title as Earl of Lucan[18].

Luttrellstown is one of the most splendid demesnes even in this county of splendid demesnes. The original house was built by Sir Thomas Luttrell, a sixteenth-century judge, and his family resided here for many generations. But the political conduct of some members of this family was so distasteful to the majority of the Irish nation, that even the family name became unpopular[19], and the name of the demesne was altered about a century ago to Woodlands. In 1891 the old name was resumed. The alteration to Woodlands was made by Luke White, the ancestor of the present owner, Lord Annaly. He was a native of the Isle of Man, who became very wealthy in Dublin. The woods of this demesne are said to have been inhabited, formerly by that Irish quadruped, the marten. Near Luttrellstown is an old house and mill called New Holland from the then popular name for Australia.

On the extreme western border of the county, where it joins the county of Kildare, there are a ruined Chapel and holy well at a place still called St. Catherine's, once a religious house of the Congregation of St. Victor[20].

Chapelizod, of which the greater portion lies north of the Liffey, derives its name from Isolde, one of the most famous heroines of the world's greatest romance. She is celebrated in the Arthurian legends and in Wagner's *Tristan und Isolde*. Isolde's Hill is believed to be the height now called Thomas's Hill where the Magazine Fort stands, and Isolde's Well is probably connected with the little stream flowing through the valley to the east of the Fort. The Parish Church of Chapelizod, dedicated to the Nativity of the Blessed Virgin, is one of the first buildings of Chapelizod passed when coming from Dublin. The tower of the Protestant Church is very old. Chapelizod is the scene of Lefanu's story, *The House by the Churchyard*, and the birthplace of Lord Northcliffe (Alfred Harmsworth). Between Farmleigh and the river is the convent of St. Joseph, founded in 1864 at Mount Sackville. It commands a splendid view of the Liffey Valley. Chapelizod was for many years the summer residence of the Irish Viceroys before the present Viceregal Lodge was acquired. In the village was the Drummond Institution, founded in 1864 by the will of Alderman John Drummond of Trinity Street, Dublin. It was for the daughters of soldiers and corresponds to the Hibernian School in the Park adjoining. The old building, called the King's House, which stood near the bridge, was purchased by Charles II from Sir Maurice Eustace as the Viceregal residence, and was inhabited for a few days by William III.

The River Liffey is at this point the headquarters of the Dublin University Boat Club, whose attractive annual regatta is held in June, when this beautiful district is at its best. The premises of the Dublin Rowing Club are on the northern bank of the river. The necessary boundary of the activities of these Clubs is the weir at Island Bridge. The present bridge is called Sarah Bridge, from the wife of a Viceroy of the end of the eighteenth century, Sarah, Countess of Westmoreland, who died at the Viceregal Lodge in 1793. The old name, Island Bridge, is from its quasi-insulated position between the rivers Liffey and Camac, or according to other accounts from its being built near an island in the river. The tide affects the Liffey up to the weir, and the river, greatly improved of late, flows on to the harbour and the sea. Dublin naturally owes its origin to its position at the mouth of the Liffey, and its name to the very black pool (Dubh Linn), not far from Grattan Bridge, where the adventurous Scandinavians, who were its real founders, anchored their ships[21].

CHAPTER III

THE TOLKA, GLASNEVIN AND THE NAUL ROAD

A LITTLE BEYOND WESTMORELAND BRIDGE the highway forks left and right. This spot was the old Cross Guns. The left or western road passes the Cemetery, founded by Daniel O'Connell. Prospect Cemetery now includes a large extent of ground on both sides of the Finglas Road, and it immediately adjoins both the Botanic Gardens and the River Tolka. Besides the Mortuary Chapel, near the road, the most conspicuous monument is the O'Connell Tower which is 168½ feet high. It was designed by Petrie, and is built of Dalkey granite. There is a story in Fitzpatrick's *History of Glasnevin Cemetery* of an exciting adventure which befell Dr. Kirwan, the City Coroner of the time. He attempted to cross the cemetery after dark, and was attacked by the bloodhounds which were still kept there by the men who watched all night. He had to stand against a tomb and defend himself until his cries brought the watchmen to his assistance. The watch-towers on the Cemetery wall are a standing memorial of those early times. A field now belonging to the Cemetery and close to the River Tolka is marked 'Bloody Acre' in ancient letters on the Ordnance Survey Maps and commemorates probably the Battle of the Wood of Tolka, fought between two Irish armies before the Norman Invasion. The maps of nearly a century ago mark a place called The Dollar opposite to the present Bengal Terrace. Farther from town on the same (west) side of the road was a house called Slut's End, which is still the name of a townland here.

The River Tolka rises in the County of Meath, about nineteen English miles from its mouth, near the railway station of Batterstown, and close to the line. Its general course is at first south-east and afterwards east. It passes Fairyhouse Station, leaves the town of Dunboyne at some distance from its right bank, and, passing through the village of Clonee, enters the County of Dublin. Having received an affluent, quaintly called the Pinkeen River, it passes Mulhuddart, near Our Lady's Well (where there is a statue of the Blessed Virgin), Blanchardstown, Lord Holmpatrick's demesne of Abbotstown with its ruined Church, Dunsinea, Ashtown, Scribblestown, Cardiff's Bridge, Finglas wood House and Bridge, Finglas Bridge, the Botanic Gardens, Glasnevin, Drumcondra, where there is another statue of the Blessed Virgin, Clonliffe, Ballybough and Annesley Bridge, North Strand, where it enters the sea. A dam has been built to confine the Tolka current to that arch of the Great Northern Railway, which immediately adjoins the East Wall or Wharf Road. Another branch of this stream has flowed hitherto through the middle arch, the central point of the railway embankment, where it crossed the sea. The valley of the Tolka, from Glasnevin to its source, exhibits some very pretty pieces of river scenery.

From Finglas Bridge the road crossing the Tolka goes on to Finglas[22], whose famous Maypole still reared itself aloft in the beginning of Victoria's reign. This village was the chief resort of the Dublin citizens on the 1st of May when May Day and Maypoles and May games were still popular. Finglas parish is dedicated to St. Canice and was a rural bishopric. Some years ago there was an old tavern sign in Finglas of Sir Thomas Picton who won the battle of Quatre Bras, and was killed at Waterloo two days afterwards. The road passes on the right the Fort or ring-mound and old Castle of Dunsoghly, belonging formerly to the Plunketts, a picturesque ruin, from the roof of which a splendid view is obtained; and farther on, Kilsallaghan Castle, the scene of a spirited defence in 1641, when 500 Irish commanded by Hugh McPhelim O'Byrne, who held it for the King, repulsed 5,000 Parliamentarians, under Sir Charles Coote, who lost 500 of his men and his ammunition and baggage. From Finglas (where a long buried High Cross was disinterred in 1816 owing to the exertions of the Rev. Robert Walsh, the Protestant curate), the road runs almost due north-west of Dublin and straight as an arrow to Ashbourne and thence to Slane and to Derry.

The eastern or right-hand road beyond Westmoreland Bridge is intersected by the Whitworth Road. This road, the Whitworth Hospital, now called Drumcondra Hospital, Whitworth Place and Whitworth Hospital Bridge and. Row in the city, are memorials of Charles, Earl Whitworth who was Lord Lieutenant 1813-17, but more famous as Ambassdor to Napoleon and France after the Peace of Amiens. In a field near Whitworth Road, John Bric, a young barrister, a native of Kerry and an ardent supporter of O'Connell, was shot dead in a duel on the morning of St. Stephen's Day, 1826, by William Hayes, a Cork Conservative. They had an accidental political dispute on Christmas Eve about an election then in progress in Cork City. The quarrel took place at the General Post Office, to which the Cork mail had just conveyed Hayes and also the news of the election. Hayes died a great many years afterwards in Cork, over ninety years of age. Whitworth Road is still popularly called the Bishop's Road, from the Right Rev, the Hon. Charles Lindsay, last Protestant Bishop of Kildare, who died in 1846. The road adjoined his property. Lindsay Road and Crawford Road (he was son of the Earl of Crawford) also commemorate this family, who are still proprietors in the neighbourhood. His sister, Lady Anne Barnard, was the author of *Auld Robin Gray*, one of the best known Scottish songs. Bishop Lindsay's residence is now the Convent of the Sisters of the Holy Faith, Glasnevin.

Passing Crawford Road and Iona Road, the new thoroughfare to Drumcondra, beside which the beautiful new Church of St. Columba is built, we reach Cody's Lane, afterwards corrupted into Corey Lane, and now called Botanic Avenue. At the corner of this road, near the little wooden Church of the Seven Dolours, there stood until 1901 a circular building which was used as a school, and said to have been founded by Dean Swift. The form, suggested by the Dean, was exactly that of an inkbottle. On the height beyond the Tolka at Bankfarm, the new Training College of the Com missioners of National Education has been built above the pond called the Roach Hole. The Botanic Garden on the left, formerly the residence of Tickell and the haunt of Addison, was founded by Dr. Wade in 1795. It had a predecessor in 1732 at Ballybough Bridge, and in 1735 at Great Martin's Lane, afterwards Mecklenburgh Street, until its transference to Glasnevin in 1795. Delville is passed next, the residence of the Very Rev. Dr. Delany, Dean of Down, whose guest Swift frequently was. Glasnevin and Finglas were also the residence of Addison, Sheridan, Southern, the author of *Oroonoko*, Tickell and Parnell.

Going farther afield, this road passes a townland called Clonmel and another called Wad. The little stream named the Holly Brook, flowing under the road at Wad Bridge passes afterwards under Doyle's Bridge at Puckstown, and Donnycarney Bridge on its course to the sea. Stormanstown is next reached, the birthplace of Mrs. Macauley, the foundress of the Sisters of Mercy, and next the Church of St. Pappan, Ballymun. This little known saint is commemorated on the same day as St. Ignatius Loyola, the Founder of the Society of Jesus, the 31st of July. Two townlands succeed, called Balbutcher and Balcurris. The prefix Bal instead of Bally (Baille) is very common in Fingal. Further on the district of Great Forest really deserved its name in former years.

Passing on we reach the Bridge of Knocksedan (the hill of the quicksand) over the Ward River, and are in quite a picturesque district. The beautiful ancient Irish circular fort at Knocksedan forms quite a remarkable and conspicuous feature. To the right is Brackenstown House, built in the reign of Charles I, the residence in older times of the Viscounts Molesworth, afterwards of the Manders family and of Mr. O'Callaghan. To the left is Killeek or Killeigh, a cemetery still used with a ruined ancient church. This district belongs to. the Staples family, baronets residing near Cookstown, Co. Tyrone[23]. The road turning west from Ballymun passes Poppintree (from St. Pappan): the Old Red Lion, once an inn, now a farmhouse; a house at the corner of the road to Dunsoghly Castle called Pass-if-you-can, a name which does not suggest strict temperance principles; the village of St. Margaret's with Church, School, Fair Green, and other rural appanages; and Chapelmidway, so called as being midway between St. Margaret's and Kilsallaghan. The main road beyond Knocksedan runs almost due north through Ballyhoghill (the town of the Staff of Jesus, St. Patrick's celebrated crozier) and the picturesquely situated village of Naul to Drogheda.

CHAPTER IV

GRATTAN BRIDGE, OLD ESSEX BRIDGE AND THE PILL

HAVING DISPOSED OF THE HIGHWAYS to Ratoath, Navan, Slane, and Naul, the next great highway on the north side of Dublin which presents itself, when passing from west to east, is the most ancient and important thoroughfare which has been for many centuries the road from Dublin to Ulster and its capital, Belfast, and the principal channel of communication with Scotland. Nowadays this road may be said to start from the City Hall and Dublin Castle, crossing the Liffey at Grattan Bridge. But this condition of the road did not begin until 1676 when Essex Bridge was built and Capel Street some years later, both receiving their names from Arthur Capel, Earl of Essex, who was Lord Lieutenant 1672-7. Arran, now the Queen's, Bridge, and Ormond, now Richmond, Bridge were built a few years later in 1683. Capel Street was the fashionable promenade of Dublin before Carlisle Bridge was built, and was the home of lottery offices as long as the State allowed them. Before the building of Essex Bridge the northern highway started, like all the roads on this side, from the only bridge over the Liffey, the Old Bridge at Church Street, and turned to the north-east at King Street and thence to the present Bolton Street.

Old Essex Bridge was a very important feature of Dublin life for more than a hundred years. It occupied the place of the present O'Connell Bridge as the principal bridge of Dublin until 1794 when Carlisle Bridge was built. It was also the bridge next the Custom House and Port, or last bridge, as Butt Bridge is now. The equestrian statue of George I, lately in the Mansion House garden, Dawson Street, was originally erected during the King's lifetime, in 1722, on old Essex Bridge, but when the restoration of that bridge was begun in 1753, the statue was removed to Aungier Street, from which it was removed in 1798 to its late position. There is an old Dublin affirmation: 'It is as true as Essex Bridge', that structure being regarded as a good type of a great concrete reality. The present bridge, named after Henry Grattan, was built on a much wider scale than Essex Bridge, and is constructed on the level system like O'Connell Bridge. It dates from 1875. The quays were embanked about 1717, and a memory of the previous condition of the riverside is preserved in the name of Strand Street, which ran by the water's edge. About 1720 were built Lower Ormond Quay, formerly Jervis Quay, and Upper Ormond Quay, the latter on the site of the Pill or Estuary of the Bradoge.

This little river which we met at Channel Row and crossed going into Stonybatter rises in Cabra, near Liffey Junction Station, close to Broome Bridge, called after William Broome, a director of the Canal Company. It flows past the junction of Faussagh Lane and Quarry Lane, lately named Connaught Street and Annamoe Road, crosses Cabra Road, passes the back of Charleville Road, along Grangegorman Lane, under the former Prison and the Broadstone Terminus, along the middle of Henrietta Street and Bolton Street, under the site of Newgate and Halston Street (Bradoge Lane), under Ormond Market, entering the Liffey at the end of East Arran Street (Boot Lane). It becomes a sewer from the spot where it enters the city proper.[24]

A street near the mouth of the river, Pill Lane, renamed Chancery Street, derived its name from the Pill or estuary of the Bradoge. Before the embankment of the Liffey in 1717 the Pill was quite a large river-inlet or harbour. The district adjoining was also called the Pill, and we read that in 1641 Charles I granted the Pill to the City of Dublin, which then lay south of the Liffey. This estuary was important at a very early period as being the 'Little Harbour of St. Mary's Abbey'[25]. In 1684 Ormond Market, now demolished, was built beside the Pill and called after James Butler, the first Duke of Ormond, who played so large a part in the history of the Stuart period both in Ireland and England. Ormond Market was long the chief home of the Dublin butchers, celebrated in Walsh's interesting *Ireland a Hundred and Twenty Years Ago* already mentioned. The butchers were Catholics, and, in the days of guilds, were the Guild of the Blessed Virgin, perhaps from their proximity to the site of her old Abbey. They waged continual warfare, the fighting taking place mostly on the bridges, with the French Protestant or Huguenot silk- weavers of the Earl of Meath's Liberties,[26] once the Liberties of the Abbey of St. Thomas a Becket. This feud did not originate, however, in difference of religion, but was the result of a dispute occurring so far back as 1607, between Oxmantown and Thomas Street, and relating to precedence in the array of the city muster.

We catch quite a picturesque glimpse of this part of Old Dublin in a passage of the Reports of the Deputy Keeper of the Records in 1424. In that year a garden is mentioned, opposite the 'Pole' water, near Oxmangreen, in the parish of St. Michan, between the land of St. Mary's Abbey on the east and the public highway (Church Street) on the west. The word Pill is of Irish origin and is the same as Peel in the Isle of Man; or Poul in Poulaphuca or Pollanass Waterfall, or Pwll in such Welsh place names as Pwllheli, Llanfairpwllgwyngyll or Braich-y-pwll. It is a pity that the new name of Pill Lane, considering the history of the name, was not Pill Street instead of Chancery Street, if the inhabitants did not like the word lane, which is disappearing fast from Dublin street-names, the name only but not, the thing. Jervis Quay and Jervis Street were called after Sir Humphrey Jervis, Lord Mayor in 1681, who obtained this part of the estate of St. Mary's Abbey as a reward for his services in building Essex Bridge with the stones of that famous old religious house, which he literally pulled down for this purpose. The Chapter House still exits, however, as an underground store. The bridge had to be rebuilt in 1755 and many believed that its comparatively rapid decay was a judgment for the impiety of Jervis, who died in a debtors' prison.

In Jervis Street was born Sir John Gilbert, who wrote the best *History of the City of Dublin*. It is, however, a History of South Dublin exclusively. Dublin north of the Liffey is altogether ignored even St. Mary's Abbey, St. Michan's Church, the Dominican Convent and Oxmantown receive no notice.

CHAPTER V

WEST OF THE GREAT NORTH ROAD

WESTWARD OF CAPEL STREET WE find Chancery Place (1825), formerly called Mass Lane, from a Church of the Jesuits, opened here in the reign of James II, but closed of necessity, like all the other Dublin Catholic churches, convents and schools, after William's victory at the Boyne. The Church then became the meeting-house of the Huguenots or French Protestant refugees then newly arrived in Ireland[27]. Mass Lane was afterwards called Golblack Lane and Lucy's Lane. The Church of St. Michan's Parish (served by the Jesuit Fathers in the penal days), to which Mass Lane led, was demolished in the course of some improvements made by the Corporation which involved the abolition of Bull Lane. Fisher's Lane, 1320, now St. Michan's Street, since 1890, was, early in the eighteenth century, the seat of three Dublin convent foundations, the Dominicans of Cabra, the Poor Clares of Harold's Cross and the Carmelites of Ranelagh. West Charles Street and Mountrath Street adjoining are called after Charles Coote, Earl of Mountrath. Greek Street and Latin Court scarcely correspond to the dignity of their names. The same remark applies to Paradise Place, Eden Garden, Angel Alley and Lucky Hall which are also to be found in our city. He who views them will be sadly disillusioned. The Presentation Convent in George's Hill close by was founded in 1794, and is the oldest Dublin foundation of that Order, which was founded by Miss Nano Nagle, who died in 1784. Little Green Street is so called since 1864 after the Little Green where Newgate was afterwards built. Halston Street was Bradoge Lane and Halfstone Street and

Beresford Street was called, from the times of Queen Elizabeth until 1774, by the singular name of Phrapper or Frapper Lane. Lord Altham resided in Phrapper Lane, and after wards in Cross Lane, Bolton Street. *Guy Mannering* is founded on the extraordinary adventures of his son James Annesley[28].

Green Street was Abbey Green in 1568; and most of the streets enumerated in this paragraph stand upon what was once the estate of St. Mary's Abbey. This celebrated religious house, first Benedictine, but after 1139 Cistercian, lay to the west of Capel Street. It is declared by some authorities to have been in existence in 908, that is well over a thousand years ago. Its church was on the north side of the street still called Mary's Abbey, a name found so far back as the year of Magna Charta. A portion of the Chapter House is still standing. Many of the streets in the neighbourhood - Mary's Abbey, Mary's Lane, Mary Street and Abbey Street - are called after this famous abbey dedicated to the Blessed Virgin. It extended on the west as far as Church Street, and is mentioned by Haliday by its old name of 'St. Mary's Abbey de Ostmanby' or of Oxman town. Its lands included on the east Terpois Park where Jervis Street now stands, the Black Ward robe, now Abbey Street, and the Ash Park, now Upper O'Connell Street. The possessions of the Abbey also included Clonliffe, Monkstown and Dunleary. St. Mary's Abbey is said to have been the scene of Silken Thomas's memorable defiance of the English Government. There is a famous old statue of the Blessed Virgin which once belonged to this Abbey and has had a most chequered history. After many vicissitudes, amongst which it served as a pig-trough, it was acquired by the late Very Rev. Dr. Spratt of the Carmelite Order, who had a genuine love for antiquity. It stands now, as the Shrine of Our Lady of Dublin, in the Carmelite Church, Whitefriars Street.

Linenhall Street and Yarnhall Street commemorate the Linen Hall, opened in 1726. The business of this Hall lay principally amongst certain important towns of Ulster, as the names of the adjoining streets recall. There are Coleraine Street, Lisburn Street, and Lurgan Street, and there was formerly Derry Street, closed to enlarge the Linen Hall in 1781. Bolton Street received its name from the Duke of Bolton, who was Lord Lieutenant 1717-21, and Dorset Street from Lionel Cranfield Sackville, the first Duke of Dorset, who was Lord Lieutenant 1731-7 and 1751-5. It had been called previously Drumcondra Lane, and we read of the Rose Tavern on the site of 38 Lower Dorset Street and the Stone Well, both on this road; as well as the Poor

Clares' Convent, subsequently the Jesuit Church and School, in Hardwicke Street, but originally opening on Drumcondra Lane.

West of Bolton Street is Henrietta Street, formerly Primate's Hill, so called from four of the Protestant Primates who resided there. Bishop's Lane and Prebend Street are still in this neighbourhood. The adjacent King's Inns were opened in 1809. The portion of the Temple Garden next the Linenhall was formerly Ancaster or Anchorite's Park, and the portion next the Broadstone was Plover Park. The valley of the Bradoge was probably once the resort of plovers. Henrietta Street derives its name from Henrietta, wife of Charles Fitzroy, second Duke of Grafton, who was Lord Lieutenant 1721-4. It contains perhaps the finest old houses on the north side of Dublin, and No. 10 was the residence of the Gardiner family, Earls of Blessington and Viscounts Mountjoy, who were the greatest owners of property on the north side. The house was built by Luke Gardiner, Vice-Treasurer of Ireland, and the family resided here for over a century. In 1874 all the Gardiner property in Dublin, except Henrietta Street, was sold in one lot for £120,000 to the Hon. Charles Spencer Cowper, son-in-law of Lord Blessington. In 1814 the first wife of the second Lord Mountjoy died, and her remains lay in state in Henrietta Street. Her funeral cost between three and four thousand pounds. The doors were thrown open, and all who would might enter and receive entertainment. This would hardly be possible now, but Dublin was then much smaller.

Upper or New Dominick Street, along with the adjoining Mountjoy Street, was built about a century ago, being much more modern than Lower or Old Dominick Street; and Blessington Street[29], called after the noble family just mentioned, is a little older, dating from 1795; but Paradise Row, called Wellington Street since the year after Waterloo, on a map, but not until 1843 in fact, is found as early as 1769. Nelson Street is a name fairly indicative of the date of the street. St. Mary's Chapel of Ease, Mountjoy Street, called the Black Church from the colour of the stone, was built in 1830. The name Eccles Street is found in 1772. It is derived from Sir John Eccles, Lord Mayor in 1710, who owned property here. His house, Mount Eccles, stood where the Loreto Convent, North Great George's Street, stands now, and he built St. George's Church, Lower Temple Street (since 1886 Hill Street) for his Protestant tenantry. Some of the Eccles family resided in the street until recent years, and they were landlords of the large house, No. 59 formerly the residence of Cardinal Cullen. At the top of Eccles Street, where the Mater

Misericordiae Hospital (opened in 1861) stands now, the Directory maps from 1796 until about thirty years later, and Byrne's Map of Dublin in 1819 mark a certain Royal Circus, whose form is indicated. It was projected but never constructed. It was to have been a splendid range of private mansions surrounding a circle instead of the usual form of a square. It was to have been approached by several grand streets, of which Eccles Street was one; and another, called Elizabeth Street, probably from Elizabeth, daughter of Sir Wm. Montgomery, Bart., and first wife of Lord Mountjoy, was to have started from Synnott Place then newly built. The Royal Circus comprised the site of St. Joseph's Church, the Mater Misericordiae Hospital, Berkeley Road and the streets west of it to the City Branch of the Royal Canal. It was intended to have included ground even beyond the North Circular Road, where Mountjoy Prison was afterwards built. The only part of it which was, in fact, made, with the exception possibly of some of the houses in Eccles Street, was Cowley Place on the North Circular Road, built in 1792 and named after Lieutenant-General Cowley who erected it[30]. The Royal Circus was projected by Lord Mountjoy, and his premature death prevented its construction. The Gardiner family had already built the splendid Sackville Street some sixty years before. Lord Mountjoy was engaged, at the time he projected this new residential district, in building Mountjoy Square[31] but the Royal Circus was to have eclipsed Merrion Square.

At the corner of Eccles Street and Berkeley Road in the plot of ground fronting the Mater Misericordiae Hospital, stands the memorial to the Four Masters, Franciscans of Donegal, an Irish Cross erected in 1876. The fine new Church of St. Joseph, Berkeley Road, was built in 1880, replacing a wooden structure erected ten years earlier. Berkeley Road was formerly called Somerset Place, and the corner house, 37 Nelson Street, Somerset House. Near St. Joseph's Church Irish national memories are recalled by the names of Geraldine Street, Fontenoy Street, Goldsmith Street, Sarsfield Street, and O'Connell Avenue[32], The beauty spots of Kerry and the south-west are similarly recalled in streets between the Circular Road and Royal Canal built fifty years ago. There are Valentia, Innisfallen, Muckross, Derrynane, Glengariff and Killarney Parades. The late Cardinal Cullen and Isaac Butt resided in Eccles Street at the same time, the first at No. 59, the second at No. 64. The latter house, conspicuous by the ornaments on its front, was the residence of Francis Johnston, the first President of the Royal Hibernian

Academy, who died in 1829. He was the architect of the Church of St. George adjoining, remarkable for its tall and beautiful spire. At one time a small square tower stood behind this house in Upper Eccles Lane. It had housed a peal of bells, the property of Johnston, who bequeathed them to St. George's Church, where they are still heard. No. 63 was the residence of Sir Boyle Roche, famous for his bulls and blunders. No. 18 Eccles Street, now part of the Dominican Convent School, was once the residence of James Cuffe, Lord Tyrawly. It was divided into two houses in 1845. It was a ladies boarding school so far back as 1835, but its present occupancy dates from 1882. Synnott Place, dating from 1795, is called after a family of that name who owned property here. Mark Synnott of Drumcondra Lane was Sheriff of the County of Dublin in 1742. This family, of Wexford origin, now resides in the County of Armagh. St. Francis. Xavier's School, next St Ignatius Road, occupies the site of an older building called Kellett's School. The present school was founded in 1850 by the late Rev. John Gaffney, S.J.

The road crosses the Royal Canal by Binns's Bridge, called, like Clarke's and Newcomen Bridges, after John Binns, one of the Directors of the Royal Canal Company in 1791. Behind the Drumcondra Hospital is St. George's Burying Ground, containing amongst other memorials the tomb of Carmichael, an eminent Dublin surgeon, from whom the well- known School of Medicine is named He was drowned on the evening of the 8th of June, 1849, in Sutton Creek while attempting to cross it on horseback from Dollymount to his residence at Sutton at low tide. The large old building facing Clonliffe Road, now the Sacred Heart Home, was previously, from 1875 to 1883, St. Patrick's Training College, which was removed in the latter year to Belvedere House beyond Drumcondra Bridge, where it still flourishes. For many years before 1875 the present Sacred Heart Home was the Convent of the Redemptoristine Nuns who removed in that year to their present convent, then newly built, on St. Alphonsus' Road named after their founder.

Saint Anne's Road adjoining was formerly called Burnett Place, but the old site was demolished a few years ago to make way for the Drumcondra Link Line Railway. The lane beside the Convent of Saint Alphonsus is called Seery's Lane. Some distance up Milibourne Avenue, formerly Mill Lane, the older Ordnance Survey Maps mark St. Catherine's Well, but all this district has been very much built over within the last fifty years. Hampstead House, on the west of the highway, was apparently named so from some analogy of its position towards Dublin with that of Hampstead Heath towards. London. Each is situated on high ground to the north commanding an extensive view of the city. The analogy was closer ninety years ago when an adjoining house was called Highgate. The name of the King's grandfather is perpetuated in the Albert Model Farm of the Commissioners of National Education lately transferred to the Department of Agriculture.

CHAPTER VI

EAST OF THE GREAT NORTH ROAD

PROCEEDING ONCE MORE FROM GRATTAN or old Essex Bridge, there are many interesting memorials on the eastern or right hand side of the great northern highway. The district on both sides of Capel Street was the property of St. Mary's Abbey. That on the eastern side, called Piphoe's Park, was purchased in 1674 by several gentlemen, including Sir Humphrey Jervis and Sir Hugh Stafford, from whom Jervis Street and Stafford Street are named. No. 44, in the latter street, the house marked with the tablet, was the birthplace of Theobald Wolfe Tone, the United Irish leader. The site of a part of the well-known and imposing Hospital (originally the Charitable Infirmary, Ormond Quay), represents No. 14 Jervis Street, the birth-place of the Volunteer Earl of Charlemont, and the residence of his step father, Thomas Adderley, who superintended his education. Mr. Adderley of Innishannon was a promoter of the linen industry in Cork. Swift's Row is called after a nephew of Dean Swift who married a daughter of Sir Humphrey Jervis. Philip Francis, whose translation of Horace is still held in high esteem, was son of the rector of St. Mary's Church, built about 1690, in Mary Street. His son was the celebrated Sir Philip Francis. Lord Langford's residence in Mary Street, afterwards the office of the Paving Board, was subsequently Bewley and Draper's establishment, and has been recently demolished. The northern portion of old Liffey Street has been called Little Denmark Street since 1773, perhaps from Caroline Matilda, Queen of Denmark, sister of George III, who died in 1775. Old St. Saviour's Church of the Dominicans from 1764 to 1858, and an

Almshouse founded in 1755 by Tristram Fortick of Fortick's Grove, afterwards Clonliffe House, are objects of interest in this street.

Simpson's Hospital[33], founded in 1781, probably gave rise to the name of Simpson's, now Sampson's, Lane, not far off. The old name was Bunting Lane. The ground extending from this lane to Henry Street was not built upon until 1790, some years after the surrounding district. It was called the Bull Park. The name of Great Britain Street, changed to Parnell Street in 1911, dates, like that of the streets already named, from the beginning of the eighteenth century, but the road is much older than the name. There was a convent of Augustinian nuns in Great Britain Street in the eighteenth century. They afterwards removed to Mullinahack near the Augustinian Church. King's Inns' Street, so called from the adjoining King's Inns since 1797, was previously named Turnagain Lane[34], apparently from the curve in the centre of the street. But old Turnagain Lane long appears on the maps as made only to Loftus Lane, where one had to turn again. The rest of the present King's Inns' Street as far as Britain Street was then covered by fields.

Lower or Old Dominick Street dates from 1743, and is called after an owner of property here who died in that year, Christopher, the son of Dr. Christopher Dominick. The association of the street with the sons of St. Dominic dates from about seventy-four years ago when the handsome Church of St. Saviour was built. Christopher Dominick's daughter Elizabeth, a very wealthy heiress, married in 1752 St. George Usher, a member of the old Dublin family, who was created Baron St. George in 1773. Lord St. George's daughter and heiress, Emily Olivia, married in 1775 the second Duke of Leinster. The Dukes of Leinster have long had an office and residence in this street. Two members of the United Irish Society of very opposite character lived on opposite sides of this street. The house No. 1, at the corner of Great Britain Street, was the residence of the honest and honourable Archibald Hamilton Rowan, whose name is associated with the history of Clongowes Wood College. In a house in Dominick Street nearly opposite lived the now notorious Leonard McNally, whose dishonour was never discovered until after his death in 1820. No. 20 was the residence of the influential John Beresford. He lived after wards in Marlborough Street and later in rooms in the new Custom House, which he caused to be built at Eden Quay. His country residence was at Abbeville, St. Dolbugh's. He was succeeded by Lord Ffrench as occupier of No. 20 in. this street. In the house, now No.

36, a few doors from Bolton Street, the famous mathematician Sir William Rowan Hamilton was born. No. 41, the Convent School of the Sisters of the Holy Faith, was for many years the town residence of the Earls of Howth. The third Earl allowed his mother-in-law, the Countess of Clanricarde, a Catholic lady, to live here. According to Fitzpatrick's *Life of Father Burke*, she wished that the house should be made a Convent of the Dominican Fathers. But when she died very old in 1854 it was purchased by the Carmelite Fathers of Whitefriars Street, who conducted a school here for a long time in which many worthy and successful citizens received their education. As the residence of Lady Clanricarde, this house figured prominently in the evidence at the great Tichborne Trial. The late Frank Thorpe Porter tells a story, in his *Recollections* about Granby Lane, the wide lane between Dominic Street and Rutland Square. William Walker, who was Recorder of Dublin from 1795 to 1822, inflicted an unusually severe sentence on a man convicted of stealing oats in that lane. The Recorder said that he was determined to put down the practice of stealing oats 'in that lane'. The fact is, that the Recorder lived in No. 11 Dominick Street and his own stable was situated in 'that lane'. Whatever malodour may have attached to the place since those earlier days has, however, been dispelled by the fact that it has become almost sacred ground, as the scene of the death of Matt Talbot, the humble Dublin workingman, whose life of martyrdom 'has become part of the history of the Church'.

At No. 12 Upper Dorset Street, Richard Brinsley Sheridan was born in 1751. His grandfather, Thomas Sheridan, a Protestant clergyman and native of Cavan, was struck off the list of chaplains to the Lord Lieutenant for preaching from the text: 'Sufficient for the day is the evil thereof', on the 1st of August, the anniversary of the accession of the King (George I) upon the death of Queen Anne. The day marked the disappearance of the Stuarts as sovereigns and the adoption by the English of the present dynasty, the House of Hanover. It is said that Sheridan was not a Jacobite, but selected his text thus awkwardly through sheer inadvertence. The name of Rutland Square dates from 1791 and comes from Charles Manners, fourth Duke of Rutland, the too jovial Lord Lieutenant who died in office in 1787, after a three years Viceroyalty. The adjoining Granby Row, an older name, comes from the title of the Duke's father, John Manners, Marquess of Granby, who did not live to succeed to the dukedom. He was one of the most famous soldiers of his time. Brave and popular, his name is well known as a cavalry commander in the Seven Years War. The north side of Rutland Square is sometimes called Palace Row from the fine house in the centre, formerly the town residence of the Earls of Charlemont, after 1871 the General Register Office, and now an Art Gallery. Palace Row is an old name, found in 1769. Cavendish Row, formerly Cavendish Street, is called after William Cavendish, the third Duke of Devonshire, who was Viceroy for the unusually long period, of eight years, from 1737 to 1745. There has been no Viceroyalty since even approaching this in length until that of Earl Cadogan, who was Lord Lieutenant from 1895 to 1902.

The first stone of the Rotunda Hospital was laid in 1751, and the adjoining grounds were called the New Gardens[35] and the Bowling Green before they received the name of Rutland Square. No. 6 Cavendish Row was the residence of Richard Kirwan, the famous chemist, a native of Galway. A great fire which consumed the block of houses where the Bethesda Church, now a cinema, is situated, occurred on the 6th of January, 1839; and it is duly chronicled in the Annals of Dublin, that the same night was that of the 'Big Wind', as the great storm continues to be called in Ireland, although it has been equalled since on the 26th of February, 1903. The lodge in the Square opposite the Presbyterian Church was a shelter for chairmen or bearers of sedan-chairs who had their stand where the cab and car stand is now. North Frederick Street dates from 1795, and probably takes its name from Frederick, Duke of York, son of George III, and many years Commander-in-Chief. Frederick Street was laid out in a district previously known for a long time as the Barley Fields. There were enough of the Barley Fields left in 1798 to hold meetings, for a popular meeting here was dispersed in that year.

Hardwicke Street should be mentioned as the first Dublin home of the Jesuits after the Restoration of the. Society, and the seat of the first Dublin College of St. Francis Xavier, the predecessor of Belvedere. It is obvious that this street and the crescent, called Hardwicke Place, as also George's Place, familiarly called 'the Pocket' from its shape, were all made with reference to St. George's Church. The Church was built in 1802, the parish having been formed in 1793 by Statute of the Irish Parliament.

The dates of the formation of the several Protestant or State Church parishes are a sufficiently good indication of the ages of the different districts of the northern half of the city of Dublin. Thus, before 1697; there was only one parish on the north side, that of St. Michan, comprising the former

Danish village of Oxmantown and the district of the Pill or mouth of the Bradoge. The Church was the very, ancient structure still standing in Church Street, erected in 1095. In 1697 by a Statute of the Irish Parliament two additional parishes were formed on the north side, that of St. Paul, of which the Church is still in North King Street, and that of St. Mary, represented by the Church in Mary Street. The latter parish received its name from the Blessed Virgin as it comprised the site and former possessions of her famous Abbey. In 1750 the parish St. Thomas was formed by Statute from the eastern district of St. Mary's. The Church, built in 1758, is in Marlborough Street. There was an older St. Thomas's Church near the Eden Quay end of the street. Lastly, St. George's Parish was formed as above mentioned in 1793.

The Catholic Church, when it had been able to emerge from the persecution of the Penal Laws, made somewhat similar arrangements. It corresponded with the Protestant Church in allocating the patronage of the first two new parishes to the Blessed Virgin and St. Paul, but no further; for St. Thomas's parish is co-extensive mainly with that of St. Laurence O'Toole, Archbishop of Dublin; and St. George's district is occupied by several Catholic parishes, those of the Blessed Virgin, St. Agatha, St. Joseph and St. Columba. Readers of this account who desire full and accurate information on the history of the development .f the parishes of the Catholic Church in Dublin and all its sacred edifices, served by the secular and regular clergy, are referred to *The Catholic Chapels in Dublin in 1749*, a very interesting pamphlet, edited and brought very fully up to date by the Most Rev. Dr. Donnelly, Bishop of Canea, and published by the Catholic Truth Society of Ireland.

St. George's Church, opened in 1802, was built by Francis Johnston, first President of the Royal Hibernian Academy of Art and an eminent Irish architect of that day[36]. He lived, as already mentioned, at 64 Eccles Street, afterwards the residence of Isaac Butt, and still adorned with sculptures on the outside. The beautiful spire of this Church is a very conspicuous landmark on the north side of Dublin; although it is now rivalled in this respect by the fine new spire of St. Peter's Church, Phibsborough, built by the Vincentian Fathers, which, however, stands upon much higher ground. St. George's, measured from the top of the cross, is two hundred feet from the ground, being sixty-six feet higher than the top of Nelson's Pillar, which, besides, is on lower ground. St. George's spire is generally seen from a distance along with that of the graceful Gothic Presbyterian Church in Rutland Square, built in 1864. The

National Gallery, Merrion Square, contains a fine view of Dublin, taken in 1853 by J. Mahoney from the spire of St. George's Church. Dubliners who visit London are often struck by the resemblance of the spire of the Church of St. Martin, near Trafalgar Square, to that of St. George in Dublin. It is evident that Johnston modelled his work to some extent on St. Martin's.

On the 10th of April, 1806, the marriage took place in this Church of the Honourable Arthur Wellesley, famous a few years later as the Duke of Wellington, with the Honourable Catherine Pakenham, daughter of Lord Longford, who resided at 10 Rutland Square. Another account states that the marriage took place in the drawingroom of the house. At No. 7 Hardwicke Place, the corner house of Hardwicke Street, the great actor, Gustavus Vaughan Brooke was born, and, under the shadow of the spire on the Church side of the street, a more famous name is to be remembered. Charles Stewart Parnell lived at No. 14 Upper Temple Street from 1862 to 1867. The house is now part of St. Joseph's Children Hospital. From the age of sixteen to that of twenty-one, Parnell passed much of his time here with his mother, brothers and sisters. During much of that time he was a student of Magdalen College, Cambridge, and afterwards held a commission as lieutenant in the militia of his native County of Wicklow. In spite of this the family were more than suspected of sympathy with the Fenians, and it was said that concealment was afforded in the house to Fenian fugitives from warrants. Mr. Barry O'Brien in his *Life of Parnell* describes the indignation of the future Irish leader when the police searched the house.

The name of Temple Street dates from 1773, and is perhaps referable to the Chapel of St. George, built, as already mentioned, by Sir John Eccles for his Protestant tenants in 1719, more than seventy years before the formation of St. George's parish. The tower of 'Little George's' looks even older than its age. Bath Lane, not far off, is called after the baths opened here in 1820 by Sir Arthur Clarke, an eminent physician who lived at No. 45 in the adjoining North Great George's Street. He was a contemporary and friend of another medical knight, Sir Charles Morgan of Kildare Street, husband of the famous Irish novelist, Sydney (Owenson), Lady Morgan. Her sister was married to Sir Arthur Clarke. A third medical knight, Sir James Murray, succeeded Sir Arthur Clarke in the medicated baths. He lived at 19 Upper Temple Street, The lane near this, running behind Belvedere House, appears on Rocque's Map of Dublin, revised by Bernard Scale, 1877, as Statute Lane. It comprised the present Graham's Court, but, unlike the latter, formed a thoroughfare from Temple Street to Frederick Street. At No. 141 Great Britain Street (Parnell) near this a well- known Irish priest and literary man was born, the late Father Charles Patrick Meehan.

North Great George's Street, whose name dates from 1776, is apparently called from its proximity to St. George's Chapel, but perhaps from George III who was then King. No. 20 was famous for its literary salon held by Sir Samuel and Lady Ferguson, who was one of the Guinness family. Major Swan, deputy to Major Sirr, lived at No. 22. They were Town Majors, a non-military title. The Earl of Kenmare resided at the present No. 35 in this street. No. 31 was the residence of Lady Catherine O'Toole, daughter of the Earl of Anglesea (Annesley) and wife of John O'Toole of Ballyfad, County Wexford, Count O'Toole and Lieutenant-Colonel of the Irish Brigade. The Loreto Convent, founded in 1837, took the place of the residence of Dr. Richard Laurence, Protestant Bishop of Cashel, an Englishman. It had been previously the residence of Sir James Galbraith, an Ulster baronet who had been a solicitor. The name of Nicholas Archdale, Esq. (whose name was originally Montgomery), is marked on old maps at this spot, evidently as residing here. Sir John Eccles's house, Mount Eccles, stood close by. Behind North Great George's Street is Johnson's Court, where there is a house facing Parnell Street, remarkable for its size and appearance in such a locality. Over the coping of the house at the corner of Great Britain Street and Cavendish Row, which preceded the National Bank, built there about thirty-six years ago, the inscription 'Raphson's Rents' appeared. For many years only the letters RAP remained over No. 2 Cavendish Row, doubtless to the perplexity of all beholders. The trustees of the Rotunda Hospital purchased ground-rents here with £800 bequeathed by one Raphson.

Gardiner's Row, dating from 1769; Gardiner Street, Upper, Middle and Lower from 1792, and Gardiner's Place, dating from 1790; Mountjoy Square (finished in 1818 from the same year; Mountjoy Street and Blessington Street, already mentioned; Great Charles Street, 1795, and Florinda Place, 1795, all take their names from the family of Gardiner, of whom the father was Lord Mountjoy[37], and the son Earl of Blessington. The mother of Lord Mountjoy was Florinda, daughter of Robert Norman of Lagore, County Meath (the Spanish name Florinda is well known in the history of Don Roderick, the last of the Goths). Great Denmark Street, so named in 1787, was originally included in Gardiner's Row. It derives its present name perhaps from Caroline Matilda, Queen of Denmark, sister of George III, who died in 1775, or from her son, afterwards Frederick VII, who became Regent in 1784.

Belvedere House, Great Denmark Street, was built about 1775, but its academic predecessor in Hardwicke Street, in turn the Church and the School of the Jesuits, has quite a green old age for this locality. Before the suppression of the Society of Jesus in 1773, we find its members ministering in the present parish of St. Michan, the Danish Bishop, and in that of SS. Michael and John. The old parish church of St. Michan's in Mary's Lane, abandoned in 1817 for Anne Street, was demolished some years ago in the course of some improvements promoted by the Corporation[38]. A very short time after the foundation of Clongowes, Father Kenny opened the Church in Hardwicke Street. The building has a singular history. Before Hardwicke Street, Frederick Street, Blessington Street or Eccles Street were yet dreamed of, or any other thoroughfare in the district, except the present Dorset Street, the old house stood there as it stands today. We hear of it first in the middle of the eighteenth century as the residence of Major Faviere, apparently a gentleman of Huguenot origin. In 1752 the Poor Clares, a part of the community of North King Street, came here, and, as they had both a convent and a chapel, curious observers may still see, by passing through Hardwicke Lane in the rear, another building, as large as that in Hardwicke Street. The Poor Clares migrated to their present home in Harold's Cross in 1803, and, about that time Beresford Street, now Hardwicke Street, was built, the houses being constructed in line with the old building. Before that time the old house is to be seen on maps, marked 'Nunnery', and opening, by an avenue through a garden, on the country road called Drumcondra Lane, now Upper Dorset Street, the only thoroughfare in the neighbourhood.

Beresford Street after a year or two received the name of Hardwicke Street from Philip Yorke, Earl of Hardwicke, Lord Lieutenant 1801-6. The Poor Clares' Convent Chapel became a chapel of ease to St. Mary's Cathedral parish, Liffey Street, served by the Rev. Bernard McMahon, until in 1816 it became the church of the Jesuits. In 1829, the year of Emancipation, the first stone of the present beautiful Church of St. Francis Xavier was laid in Upper Gardiner Street, and it was opened in 1832. Then the house in Hardwicke Street became the College of St. Francis Xavier as it had previously been his Church. The name of the Saint is commemorated in a little avenue off the North Strand, as is that of St. Ignatius in a road off Dorset Street, both names being obvious tributes to the Jesuit 'sphere of influence'.

The advertisements of the School and its Course are to be found in the earlier editions of the *Irish Catholic Directory*, and they seem a little old-fashioned to us of the present day. From the same authority for 1842 we learn that the new College of St. Francis Xavier was opened in Belvedere House on the 16th of September, 1841. In connection with the history of the house, we may recall the facts that the earldom of Belvedere, created in 1756, was held but by two peers, father and son, when it became extinct in 1814 on the death of the latter. His widow, Jane, daughter of the Rev. James Mackay of Phibsborough, married Mr. Abraham Boyd, K.C., and died in 1836; and the names of the Countess of Belvedere and her son, Mr. G.A. Boyd, are those returned as occupiers of the house in the Dublin Directories before the foundation of the College in 1841[39].

In the Belvedere School district the name is preserved in Belvedere Place and Belvedere Road, both leading from Mountjoy Square to another school of St. Francis Xavier. There are also the little Belvedere Avenue, called until 1875 North East Anne Street, a complex name; Belvedere House, now St. Patrick's Training College, formerly the residence of the Coghills, baronets, now residing in County Cork; and Belfield Park, Drumcondra, called from the Belvedere minor title, Viscount Belfield; and for some years the residence of the late A.M. Sullivan.

Belvedere House is the best preserved of the splendid old Dublin houses of the Georgian period. At that time the fine new houses built in this part of Dublin were taxed according to the length of their frontage. It was built about 1775 by George Rochfort, second Earl of Belvedere, at a cost of £24,000. The first Lord Belvedere purchased the site in 1765 from Nicholas Archdale who held a lease from the Eccles family of Mount Eccles. Mount Eccles stood almost on the site of the present Loreto Convent in North Great George's Street, and Mr. Archdale resided there about the time when Belvedere House was built. He was originally Nicholas Montgomery, but assumed the surname of Archdale upon his marriage with a lady of that family. The grand organ which had belonged to the Belvedere family is still preserved in the College in a case of fine San Domingo mahogany. The ornamentation by Lord Belvedere's Venetian artists was restored by the Jesuit Fathers a quarter of a century ago. The plaster reliefs on the walls and ceilings, the Bossi marble chimney pieces, and the three rooms whose decoration was dedicated to Apollo, Venus and Diana respectively, are now in as good condition as they were a century ago, and afford, as has been said, the best surviving example of eighteenth-century splendour in Dublin house decoration.

The success of Belvedere College as an educational institution is known to everybody. Many most distinguished Irishmen were educated here, and some who still survive are not the least famous[40]. The house No. 5 Great Denmark Street, next to Belvedere House and formerly the town residence of the Earls of Fingal, has been attached to the College since 1880. The extensive new buildings of the College, including the boys' chapel, class rooms and science laboratories, were erected in 1884. The large gates in Great Denmark Street bear the arms of St. Ignatius.

An anecdote may well be inserted here of a famous Irish writer who went to school in Great Denmark Street. Charles Lever was born in Amiens Street and lived afterwards in Talbot Street, both on this side of Dublin. He went to a school at No. 2 Great Denmark Street, kept by the Rev. George Newenham Wright, who brought out a *Guide to Dublin* in 1821. The boys of Wright's School, having a dispute with those of another school in Grenville Street (then very fashionable), agreed to settle it by a pitched battle in Mountjoy Fields, on a part of which the Church of St. Francis Xavier, Upper Gardiner Street, now stands. So elaborate was the fight that the Denmark Street boys actually laid a mine. When the mine was fired many on both sides were injured and the leaders found themselves in custody. The guardians of the peace brought them to the long extinct Marlborough Street Police Office, where Lever, chosen as spokesman and apologist, so pleased the magistrate by the wit and cleverness of his explanation as to secure the discharge of all concerned.

No. 1 Great Denmark Street was the residence of Lord Tullamore, afterwards Earl of Charleville. No. 3 was the town house of the well-known Earl of Norbury the judge, who has been already mentioned at Cabra. No. 4 was the mansion of the Creighton family, Earls of Erne, whose memory is perpetuated in the names of Creighton Street and Erne Street on the south side of Dublin, on property acquired by them through marriage with the heiress of Sir John Rogerson, after whom the quay is named. No. 7, next door to Belvedere College, was the residence of Sir Robert King, Bart. No. 8 was the residence of Lady Hannah Stratford, sister to the Earl of Aldborough, who built Aldborough House[41].

Grenville Street, 1792, and Buckingham Street, Marquess of Buckingham, who was Lord Lieutenant 1782-3 and 1787-9. But Temple Street can hardly have received its name from him, as the name is found in 1773, and he was not associated with Ireland until nine years later. At No. 44 Mountjoy Square (South) Dr. Daniel Murray, Archbishop of Dublin, lived for twenty-five years previous to his death on the 26th of February, 1852[42]. No. 53 (formerly 74) Upper Gardiner Street was for some years the residence of Denis Florence McCarthy, the poet. It stands at the corner of Sherrard Street, dating from 1795, and called after Mr. Thomas Sherrard, Secretary of the Commissioners of Wide Streets. No. 3 Lower Sherrard Street was the residence of the Rev. James Wills, well known for his services to Irish literature, and father of William Gorman Wills, the dramatist. The Jesuit Fathers of St. Francis Xavier's Church inhabited the present No. 38 Upper Gardiner Street for a few years before the residence beside the Church was built.

The Church of St. Francis Xavier in Upper Gardiner Street is in the classical style and richly decorated. The fine Ionic portico is much admired. The first stone was laid by Father Charles Aylmer, S.J., on the 2nd of July, 1829, the year of Emancipation, and it was opened on the 3rd of May, 1832, replacing the Church in Hardwicke Street where the celebrated Father Peter Kenny had long preached and ministered. St. Francis Xavier's in Gardiner Street was designed by Father Bartholomew Esmonde, S.J., and erected by the architect Joseph B. Keane, who also built St. Laurence O'Toole's Church, Seville Place. The erection of Gardiner Street Church cost £25,000.

Cardinal Cullen lived at No. 3 Belvedere Place in the beginning of his Episcopate. Belvedere Place dates from 1795 and Fitzgibbon Street from 1794. The latter is called after John Fitzgibbon, Earl of Clare. Portland Street and Portland Place date from 1811 and are called after the third Duke of Portland, who was Prime Minister 1807-9, and had been Lord Lieutenant in 1782. Russell Place and Russell Street are called after John Russell who built them in 1792. The Christian Brothers School, North Richmond Street, dates from 1828, but the street is marked on maps of about fourteen years earlier. Daniel O'Connell laid the foundation stone of the school on St. Columba's Day, the 9th of June, 1828. The 5th of July following was polling-day in the Clare election, the result of which ensured the achievement of Catholic Emancipation. Gerald Griffin, the famous Irish poet and novelist, became a member of the Order of the Christian Brothers and taught for some time in

53

this school. Many very eminent men have been pupils of O'Connell's School, which has become quite famous for its unfailing success in the Intermediate Examinations. Richmond Place adjoining dates from 1818, and takes its name, like Richmond Bridewell, Asylum, Penitentiary, Barracks and Hospital, from Charles, fourth Duke of Richmond[43].

Wellesley Place, off Russell Street, is named after Richard Colley Wellesley, Marquess Wellesley, also famous as a soldier. He was twice Lord Lieutenant, had been Governor-General of India and was eldest brother of the Duke of Wellington. A large old house stood, until quite recent years, in Lower Dorset Street, a little to the north of the Circular Road. Near it was the Big Tree which disappeared many years before the house.

Clonliffe Bridge, connecting Jones's Road with Russell Street, is of somewhat later date than any other Royal Canal bridge in Dublin. Unlike all the rest, it bears no stone indicating its name and date, and has an iron railing instead of a stone parapet; but Russell Street at first ran towards the water's edge. The juxtaposition of Fitzroy Avenue and Buccleuch Villas, Jones's Road, which is merely accidental, recalls the marriage in 1663 of James Fitzroy, Duke of Monmouth with Anne Scott, Countess, afterwards Duchess, of Buccleuch in her own right. She is the Duchess introduced in *The Lay of the Last Minstrel*. But Fitzroy Avenue here was called after a street of the same name in Belfast. The name Edgar Villas on this road is from the first owner of the property.

Jones's Road represents a former foot-path through the fields leading to the gate of Clonliffe House, still standing on the College grounds, the residence a century ago of Fredereick Edward Jones, the manager of the principal theatre in Dublin. Clonliffe Road, in its present long straight form, is not much more than a century old. It was pre ceded by a narrow winding lane called Fortick's Lane, from Tristram Fortick, then residing in Clonliffe House which was called Fortick's Grove. It was Jones who restored the Irish name to the house and estate. Clonliffe is translated 'meadow of herbs' by Dr. Joyce, but 'plain of the Liffey' by Cardinal Moran, who thinks the district once extended as far as the Liffey. It was a part of the great possessions of St. Mary's Abbey. It is at present divided into three townlands. Clonliffe South lies between the Royal Canal and North Circular Road. Clonliffe West between the Tolka and the Canal to the west of Drumcondra Road, and Clonliffe East to the east of that highway, extending as far as Ballybough Bridge. Drumcondra has usurped the place of Clonliffe as the name of the district[44]. The true Drumcondra is beyond the Tolka.

'Buck' Jones, the most celebrated possessor of Clonliffe House, was a native of Meath. During his occupation of the house, one or two noteworthy incidents took place there. A barrister named Comerford, a guest of Jones, had a presentment that he would be drowned in the Canal when returning to town from Clonliffe. Notwithstanding this he continued to go home by the path from the gate to the water's edge which preceded Jones's Road, instead of going round by either of the next two canal bridges which existed then as now. He was drowned. Another tragic incident, characteristic of the times in Ireland, but resembling what we read sometimes of the Western States, occurred on the 6th of November, 1806. Jones, an active magistrate, attempted to capture Larry Clinch, a highwayman who had attacked, robbed and burnt an Ulster mail-coach at Santry. It is said that Jones refused the offer of Clinch's wife to betray her husband to him. But Jones received warning that the robber and his men intended to attack Clonliffe House. He secured a guard of the Tipperary Militia under an officer, Lieutenant Hamerton. The attack took place in due course, and after the exchange of many shots, the robbers were worsted, two of them being killed. Their dead bodies were expose; but, as their friends feared to claim them, they were buried at the Ballybough end of Clonliffe Road. This is the foundation of a ghost story which has always prevailed in the locality.

But the pretty poem of *The Ghost's Promenade* by the late Thomas Caulfield Irwin, is quite a different and a much older story. The romantic and tragic episode narrated in the poem probably never had a 'local habitation and a name', save in the brain of the poet, although he lays the scene in Clonliffe House. Irwin's picture of Clonliffe Road will surprise those who know it in its present condition.

> *There was a long old road anear the*
> *Skirted with trees*
> *One end joined a great highway, one led down*
> *To open shores and seas.*
> *There was no house upon it saving one,*
> *Built years ago.*
> *Dark foliage thickly blinded from the sun*
> *Its casements low.*

After Jones's time Clonliffe House became an auxiliary Feinaglian School to Aldborough House, of which we shall speak further on. It was then from 1845 to 1857 a barrack of the Revenue Police, a force long extinct. On the feast of the Finding of the Holy Cross, the 3rd of May, 1860, Archbishop, afterwards Cardinal, Cullen, laid the first stone of Holy Cross College. The foundation had been begun in Clonliffe House on the 14th of September, 1859. This fine building, with its beautiful chapel, built some sixteen years later, completely dwarfs the old house. The Most Rev. Dr. Walsh, Arch bishop of Dublin, built his residence on the College grounds about the year 1890. The Swords road was cut through the hill at this point in 1817. One of the last turnpikes in Dublin still existed up to 1850 on the northern highway, almost opposite the point where St. Alphonsus Road now intersects it. The adjoining lane was called Turnpike Lane long after the unpopular obstruction disappeared.

Richmond Road and Avenue north of the Tolka are not called after the Duke of Richmond already mentioned, but take their names from the adjoining townland of Richmond, the name of which is to be found long before the time of his Viceroyalty. Bernay Lodge on this road is called after a town in Normandy, and Bushfield, in Philipsburgh Avenue adjoining, was formerly named Cutaldo[45]. The townland north of Richmond is called Goosegreen, probably after Goose Green south-east of London, near Peckham Rye, and the road running through it from Richmond is called Goosegreen Avenue, but the southern extremity was named Gracepark Road about twenty-five years ago. Drumcondra was the scene of the historic marriage of Hugh O'Neill and Mabel Bagenal. This district contains so many religious institutions, that it has acquired the name of 'the Holy Land'. But the townland of Puckstown, where it is connected with the high road by the short turn called the Yellow Lane, takes it name from an ancient Irish spirit who has scarcely the note of sanctity. The Black Bull Inn was in Puckstown. It stood on the right of the high road, a little to the Dublin side of the Yellow Lane. The churchyard adjoining Drumcondra Protestant Church contains the graves of Furlong, Gandon and Grose. The first, a native of Scarawaish, County Wexford, was apprenticed when young to a Dublin grocer, where, no doubt, he saw such incidents as he describes in his poem of *The Drunkard*, which opens:

> *Along Drumcondra Road I strolled,*
> *The smoky town was just in sight.*

The tale is as true to-day as it was a century ago. This promising poet died young in 1827, and did not live to see Catholic Emancipation, in the struggle for which he had borne an active part. James Gandon was architect of some of the finest buildings in Dublin, including the Four Courts[46]. Francis Grose, the eminent antiquary, was a friend of Gandon. Church Lane, where this churchyard is situated, has a row of cottages long called Belvedere Place, evidently from Belvedere House adjoining, now St. Patrick's Training College. On maps of more than a century ago there is a house marked on Drumcondra Road, opposite Belvedere House, called Fitzpatrick's Lodge. Corpus Christi Church, on Home Farm Road, was built to serve the new suburb of Upper Drumcondra. White Hall takes its name from a former resident, Richard White, grocer, of Gloucester Place.

The road parallel to the highway on the east, reaching a spot once called Cold Harbour, terminates at Beaumont, now a Convalescent Home of the Mater Misericordiae Hospital, but formerly the residence of two Arthur Guinnesses, father and son, the great grandfather and the grandfather of Lords Ardilaun and Iveagh. The elder Arthur, was the founder of the famous firm. The little stream, called the Naniken River, which rises near Beaumont, flows into the sea at St. Anne's. The Missionary College of All Hallows, founded in 1842, is in the townland of Drumcondra, which belonged, like Baldoyle, to the ancient Priory of All Hallows, which stood where Trinity College stands now. Drumcondra and Baldoyle were granted, at the dissolution of the monasteries, to the Corporation of Dublin. The last occupier of Drumcondra House before All Hallows College was founded there was Sir Guy Campbell, Bart., a distinguished soldier, who was married to Pamela, daughter of Lord Edward Fitzgerald. Mr. George Wyndham was a grandson of Sir Guy and Lady Campbell.

CHAPTER VII

THE GREAT NORTH ROAD AND FINGAL

THOSE WHO TRAVEL BY THE main roads on the north side of Dublin may remark that the country proper is more immediately accessible on this side of the city than on the south. Beyond Drumcondra the highway passes through the pretty village of Santry, built in 1840 by the Lady Domville of the day, on a Swiss model. It is an agreeable change from the usual form of a County Dublin village. Outside it is a house called Magenta Hall from the place in the north of Italy where Marshal McMahon and the French, with whom Napoleon III was present, gained a victory over the Austrians on the 4th of June, 1859. One of the many houses called Royal Oak is at Santry. It was evidently an inn. The road beside it, leading to Coolock, is called Santry Lane on old maps. Santry Court, beside the village, is one of the finest demesnes near Dublin with a Jacobean mansion. It was the residence of the Barry family, who, having become wealthy by commerce in Dublin, were created Lords Barry of Santry. Newtownbarry in Wexford was called after one of these Barrys. Many stories are current of the wild freaks of one member of this family. The Domvilles succeeded to the estate through intermarriage with the Barrys and afterwards it passed to the Pocklingtons, an English family, who assumed the name of Domville. From them the present baronet is descended. Santry Court is now occupied by Captain Poë, who is related by marriage to the Domville family.

The highway, passing through the townland of Tubberbunny, or the Well of the Milk, crosses the Cuckoo Stream which, rising near Collinstown, flows through St. Dolough's and into the sea at Portmarnock, as the Mayne

River. The Santry River, nearer to Dublin, flows through Raheny into the sea at Watermill Bridge. The next village is Cloghran, which is on a height, and some miles farther the ancient town of Swords is reached. Swords was dedicated to St. Columbkill, and still possesses many remains of antiquity, as the Round Tower, residence of the Archbishops, and Glasmore Abbey where St. Cronan and his monks are said to have been massacred by the Danes more than a thousand years ago. Richard Montgomery, the brave and capable soldier of the War of American Independence, was born at Feltrim near Swords. Swords recalls the north of Italy more forcibly even than Magenta Hall near Santry ; for it has a house called Mantua on the north-east and another called Cremona on the south-west. There is also Meudon but there is no Rabelais.

Swords had two members in the Irish Parliament, and was altogether a more important place than Donabate, although the latter has now a station on the Great Northern Railway and occupies the proud position of capital of the peninsula of Portrane, for Donabate is certainly bigger than Ballisk. This peninsula, enclosed between Rogerstown Creek and Malahide Creek (the latter formed by the confluence of the Ward and Broad Meadow Rivers) was formerly noted, it is said for the manufacture of poteen, but is now better known for its great Asylum and for the memorial tower on the coast to Mr. George Evans of Portrane House, erected by his widow, one of the Parnell family. In 1771 the excise officers captured from smugglers at Portrane, seventy-five chests and twenty casks of tea, and one hundred and eleven casks of brandy, and eight hundred casks of tea and brandy in the 'Island of Donabate' (probably Lambay or Portrane Peninsula) all in one seizure. The excisemen stored their capture in barns, and were besieged there for twenty-four hours by five hundred armed smugglers, and relieved at last by Captain Luske and his crew, whose warship happened to be off the coast. The sailors landed and defeated the smugglers.

Off Portrane lies Lambay Island, 1,371 acres in extent, according to D'Alton, but 595 acres 3 roods on the Ordnance Map; it is, however, the largest on the east coast of Ireland. It has a tidal harbour, a castle built in the reign of Mary Tudor, a wood, something resembling a village, several high hills a spring called Trinity Well, where there used to be a 'pattern' on Trinity Sunday, and a glen rejoicing in the romantic name of Thorn Chase Valley. For centuries the property of the Talbots of Malahide, it has recently passed out of their possession, and, although there are some very tragic stories of poor prisoners who were 'marooned' and starved to death on Lambay, it is more usual now for people to be kept off rather than on.

Enterprising cyclists may, if they choose, take the road from Swords to Balbriggan. It passes through Ballough and by the hill called the Man of War, which is about equally far north with the Nag's Head on the Naul Road, or the village of Garristown. Farther on it passes near the Bog of the Ring, which would seem a freak of Fingallian nomenclature if there were not many other names as odd[47]. The road passes through the village and barony of Balrothery to Balbriggan, famous for its hosiery, where there is a very fine strand, and thence to the Delvin River, the boundary of the County of Dublin, and of the ancient district of Fingal which stretches southwards to the Tolka.

But if the cyclist takes the right-hand turn at Coldwinters beyond Swords he finds himself in the true home of the Fingallians, the coast district, including Rush and Lusk, Loughshinny and Skerries The Fingallians are said to be different in features, voice and manner from the other people of Leinster and this difference may be ascribed to their Scandinavian origin. They are good farmers, Sailors and fishermen and have many good qualities. A recent lady writer extols their cleanliness and excellent housewifery. The villages of North County Dublin are said to be cleaner than those in the south of the county. Lusk has a very fine specimen of a Round Tower. But some may prefer to visit the smuggler's cave at Rush, the resort of the eighteenth-century smuggler, Jack Connor, called Jack the Bachelor, who lies buried in Rush churchyard. Luke Ryan, who commanded the *Black Prince* privateer under French auspices during the American War of Independence, was a native of Rush. One episode of his daring career was his trial on four different occasions for piracy. He was sentenced to be executed and gibbeted, but the sentence was never carried out. In Rush churchyard is the tomb of Sir Robert Echlin, Bart., of Kenure. D'Alton quotes the lines of this tomb, but does not seem to know that they are from two of Pope's best Epitaphs[48], apparently appropriated by the person who erected the monument.

Outside Rush is Kenure Park, the residence of Sir Roger Palmer, Bart., who was a Lieutenant-General retired. He took part in the Balaklava charge, and survived it by fifty-six years. He was lineally descended from Miss Ambrose, Lord Chesterfield's 'dangerous Papist'. The other fine demesnes in this part of the county are Hacketstown[49], Milverton, Ardgillan and Hampton. Baldungan

Castle, an interesting ruin, belonged to the Knights Templars, and afterwards to the De Berminghams and the Howth family. The Church here is of the Norman period. Balrothery Castle belonged to the Barnewalls. The neat town of Skerries, a fishing village a few years ago, is now well known as a summer resort. Beyond the group of islands from which it is called, and far out at sea lies the wild rock with the lighthouse called Rockabill, or, on older maps, the Rock of Bill. Rockabill would be an ideal scene for a picture of a storm.

CHAPTER VIII

THE CENTRE OF THE NORTH CITY

HAVING DISPOSED OF THE GREAT northern highway the next thoroughfare to be traversed in the northern half of Dublin is the finest street in the city, and one of the finest in the world. It was proposed in 1884 that the name of Sackville Street should be changed to O'Connell Street, and this proposal was carried into effect eventually. The street first appears, as Drogheda Street, early in the eighteenth century, a narrow thoroughfare extending from the country road to Clontarf, called first Ballybough Lane and afterwards Great Britain Street from 1720 to 1911, and since then Parnell Street, to Abbey Street near the river, where there was no bridge until the end of that century; there was, however, a ferry at this point. Drogheda Street and several streets adjoining were called from Henry Moore, Earl of Drogheda. The full list is Henry Street, Moore Street, North Earl Street, Of Lane, afterwards Off Lane and now Henry Place, and Drogheda Street[50]. Charles, second Earl of Drogheda, died in 1679 in his new house in North Earl Street. The old Dublin residence of the family was in Mary's Abbey.

In Rocque's Map of Dublin, 1756, the name Drogheda Street is confined to the narrow old street running from Henry Street and Earl Street, the southern corners of which two streets were then quite close to each other, to Abbey Street close to the riverside; while the fine new wide street from the New Gardens (Rutland Square) and newly-built Hospital to the site of Nelson's Pillar was called Sackville Street. The name was taken from Lionel Cranfield Sackville, the first Duke of Dorset, who was Lord Lieutenant from 1731 to 1737 and from 1751 to 1755. The assertion has been sometimes made, but without any reasonable foundation, that the name came from that of the Duke's younger son, Lord George Sackville, who, although a man of ability, incurred some discredit as he was accused of cowardice or insubordination at the Battle of Minden in 1759. But he had not attained to much fame, good or bad, when the name was conferred on the new street. The old, or Drogheda Street, side of the street, is the eastern side as it was widened by extending it westward.

Old Drogheda Street was widened from the New Gardens to where the Pillar stands now, and the name of Sackville Street was conferred on the splendid new street by the Right Hon. Luke Gardiner (grandfather of the first Lord Mountjoy), who did so much to improve and beautify the north side of Dublin, Gardiner had purchased this estate from" the Drogheda family. The long unbroken row of more than thirty houses, from Britain Street to Henry Street, forming the new western side, was called Gardiner's Mall. A mall or walk ran in the centre of the street, just as such a walk runs now in the centre of O'Connell Bridge. The fine new street, containing the most beautiful private residences in Dublin, must have been quite an attractive place. It was the last suburb on this side, for Great Britain Street was the country. Almost the whole of Dublin was on the southern side of the Liffey; and the nearest bridge, by which this point could be reached, until the end of the century, was Essex Bridge, a long way off. No. 10 Sackville Street, on the old aide, was the residence of the Earl of Drogheda, and many other noblemen resided in the street. About the year 1840 the famous musician Logier lived at the present No. 50, now Messrs. Gill's, and the Dorset Institution, a few doors away, commemorates a successor of the Duke of Dorset from whose surname the street derived its name.

The opening of the new Custom House in 1791 brought about great changes in this part of Dublin. Carlisle Bridge, joining Sackville Street with College Lane, now Westmoreland Street, named after another Viceroy, was built in 1794 and did not give place to the present splendid O'Connell Bridge until 1880[51]. It ceased to be the last bridge, or bridge next Dublin Harbour, in 1879, when Butt Bridge was built and called after Isaac Butt, who died at Roebuck on the 5th of May in that year. The adjoining Loop Line Railway Bridge was erected in 1891. Shortly after the opening of Carlisle Bridge the remaining piece of Drogheda Street was widened westward like the upper or northern portion, by the Wide Streets Commissioners[52], and the whole street from the Rotunda to the bridge was called Sackville Street.

The column to the memory of Nelson, which is one hundred and thirty-four feet high, was erected in 1808, the foundation stone having been laid by the Duke of Richmond, Lord Lieutenant, on the 15th of February in that year. It is said to have been designed by William Wilkins of Norwich, but the statue of Nelson is by an Irish sculptor, Thomas Kirk, R.H.A. Nelson's Pillar was erected by public subscription and cost £6,856. It was profusely decorated with flags on the centenary of Trafalgar. For a very long time the project of removing the Pillar, which many condemn as an obstruction to traffic, has been mooted, but it has never taken definite shape. The Pillar is a fluted Doric column with a spiral staircase inside, and openings for light. A fine view is obtained from the top. A few years after the Pillar came the General Post Office, a work of Francis Johnston, as another new feature of the district, and, in 1809, apparently because the new Pillar began to be recognized as a landmark, Sackville Street was divided into Upper and Lower, starting from this point[53]. The Pillar looked much better when newly-erected than it does now after the smoke of a century. Immediately after its erection, its mountain granite surface was of a dazzling white.

Carlisle Bridge was the scene of many executions in 1798; amongst others of that of Dr. John Esmonde who lived in the County of Kildare. His eldest son inherited the family baronetcy and another was a respected Jesuit, Father Bartholomew Esmonde, who died in 1862. The majestic statue of Daniel O'Connell, the Liberator, was unveiled on the 15th of August, 1882, a Volunteer centenary. It was cast by the great sculptor, John Henry Foley, who was born in No. 6 Montgomery Street, not far off, on the 24th of May, 1818. The statue of Sir John Gray was unveiled in 1879. He was instrumental in giving Dublin its present fine water supply and was for many years proprietor of the *Freeman's Journal*, which was carried on from 1763 to 1924. It was founded by Lucas. The statue is by the late Sir Thomas Farrell, who was born in Mecklenburgh Street, also in this part of Dublin[54]. On the north side of the Pillar the statue of Father Theobald Mathew, the Apostle of Temperance, was unveiled in 1893. It was sculptured by Miss Mary Redmond and represents him in his Capuchin habit. At the northern end of the street, next to the Rotunda, the memorial has been erected to Charles Stewart Parnell. It is by Augustin St. Gaudens, a sculptor who is classed as an American, but was born in Dublin of a French father and Irish mother. This monument will be probably the last of the range of memorials in the centre of this fine street.

Sackville Place and Lane in this neighbourhood bear names of similar origin to that of the street, as also does Mount Sackville, the finely situated residence at Knockmaroon, now well known as St. Joseph's Convent. But Sackville Garden and Sackville Avenue, which are not very far from the street, have a different origin. Sackville Place was formerly Tucker's Row, and was for some time called Mellifont Lane, from Mellifont Abbey, a famous religious house which was afterwards the residence of the Earls of Drogheda. Cole's Lane seems to derive its name from the maiden name of one of the earlier Countesses of Drogheda. From this lane to Moore Street an extinct street called Greg Street ran a hundred and seventy years ago. It seems to be represented nowadays by Riddall's Row.

Nelson Lane (re-named Earl Place in 1896) and Nelson Street date from a year or two after the erection of the Nelson Column. Moore Lane, running behind Gardiner's Mall, was called, up to 1773, Brickfield Lane, and there were really brickfields there, a thing not to be easily realized from its present aspect. From this runs Sackville Lane, and off it there is a lane bearing the extraordinary name of Cadslough. The name has been in the Directories for many years, and is to be found on maps of more than ninety years ago. The depression in the ground seems to indicate that there was a 'lough' there once, like the Yellow Pool or Lough Buoy, now called Bow Street, off North King Street.

Elephant Lane, leading to Marlborough Street, was apparently named from a shop or mart called the Elephant. We read, in a Dublin trial in 1821, of purchases made at 'Chebsey's of the Elephant in Sackville Street'. There has been a house bearing an image of an elephant for many years in another part of the street, near the corner of Middle Abbey Street. But the name Menagerie Lane is found on old maps near Elephant Lane[55]. The latter became Tyrone Place in 1870 as it leads to Tyrone House; but, as this old Irish name was appropriated by the neighbouring Mecklenburgh Street more than forty years ago, Tyrone Place was changed to Cathedral Street in 1900 - three names in thirty years.

It runs by the Pro-Cathedral, of which the first stone was laid in 1815 in Marlborough Street on the site of the town mansion of the Earls Annesley. When the Cathedral was opened in 1826, the old Church in Liffey Street, behind Bewley and Draper's, then the Paving Board, was deserted. Both Metropolitan Churches were dedicated to the Blessed Virgin. During the building of the Cathedral the Most Rev. Dr. Troy, Archbishop of Dublin, took up his residence at 3 Cavendish Row; and his Coadjutor and ultimate successor, the Most Rev. Daniel Murray, resided in Cumberland Street from 1815 to 1827 in the house next to Mecklenburgh Lane, afterwards No. 39. The present condition of the neighbourhood of the last-mentioned house affords a striking indication of the decay of Dublin within the old city boundary.

Before Drogheda Street, Moore Street and Of Lane were laid out the fields there bore the name of the Ash Park, being one of the 'parks' of St. Mary's Abbey, seemingly named from ash-trees which grew there. Terpois Park occupied the site of Jervis Street; and that known as the Black Wardrobe of Middle Abbey Street. North Prince's Street is nearly two hundred years old, and its name is probably derived from the Prince of Wales, afterwards George II. Lower Ormond Quay was Jervis Quay. Bachelor's Walk and Lane and (formerly) Bachelor's Quay seem to derive their names from some long deceased capitalist called Batchelor. Bachelor's Walk formerly included a part of what is now Eden Quay. No. 11 Bachelor's Walk was the residence of Captain John Neville Norcott D'Esterre, a Town Councillor and ex-officer in the Navy, mortally wounded by O'Connell in a duel at Bishopscourt near Naas, on the 1st of February, 1815. The back lane here called Lots seems to be quite unchanged since it was made. The name is from the 'lots' drawn by which reclaimed land here was distributed.

CHAPTER IX

THE OLD ROAD TO THE SEA

G REAT BRITAIN STREET, SINCE 1911 Parnell Street, Summer Hill and Ballybough Road are a very old thoroughfare, but were quite rural until about the middle of the eighteenth century, when houses and intersecting streets began to be built. This was the old road to the sea, and Ballybough Lane, the predecessor in title of Ballybough Road, was the coast road before the building of Annesley Bridge in 1797. Ballybough Bridge, where this old highway crosses the Tolka, was built so far back as 1308 by a benevolent and public-spirited Provost of Dublin, John le Decer. His office was equivalent to that of Lord Mayor. Decer's bridge was swept away by a flood in 1313 and the present dates from 1488, being one of the oldest bridges in Dublin.

Before a bridge was built here, the Tolka was crossed by 'the fishing-weir of Clontarf', which plays such a prominent part in the Battle of Clontarf. We are told that many of the pagan enemy were killed at this old Danish weir, and that many were drowned in the Tolka, the tide being at its flood at five minutes before six o'clock on that day. The road or path from Dublin to this weir, started in those days like all the North County roads from the present Church Street, and the 'ford of the hurdles', where the first bridge was afterwards built. 'The Liffey was then un-confined, and spread out widely, and the sea flowed over the space where now stand the Custom House, Amiens Street, the Northern Railway Terminus, and all the adjacent streets lying between them and the sea. The main battle ground extended from about the present Upper O'Connell Street to the River Tolka, and beyond along the shore towards Clontarf. The Danes stood with their backs to the sea; the Irish on the land side facing them.'[56]

Dr. John Brennan, more famous as a literary man than as a physician, lived at No. 192 Great Britain Street. No man could be more vitriolic in his writings and words, and his poem on the four provinces of Ireland is unequalled in bitterness. His epigram on a brother physician in Dublin was

> *Name the grave you wish, to be buried in*
> *Before you send for Dr. Sheridan.*

Summer Hill, formerly known as Farmer's Hill, contained many fine residences a hundred years ago. Lord Ffrench lived here and some other Irish peers. There are rows of very large old houses on the eastern side of the street, especially between Rutland Street and Buckingham Street. Though not much of a hill, the rising ground is quite apparent. The steep piece of waste ground in Lower Rutland Street on which the school is now built, has long been popularly called Bunker's Hill; nor was this the only memorial of American Independence in the district; for the little street called Buckingham Place was Washington Street early in the nineteenth century, and there was also a Washington Row here.

Langrishe Place was the property of Sir Hercules Langrishe, Bart., of Knocktopher, a member of the Irish Parliament, who died in 1811. Like Luke Gardiner, Lord Mountjoy, his Dublin neighbour, Sir Hercules, was an advocate of Catholic Emancipation, which not even Lucas, Charlemont and Foster were prepared to concede. Hutton's Lane, now Place, is called after the old Dublin firm whose factory adjoined it. There was a place off Summer Hill punningly called Lane's Lane. John Cornelius O'Callaghan, author of the *Irish Brigade in the Service of France* and the *Green Book,* lived in Upper Rutland Street, as did George Petrie at 21 Great Charles Street. The short new street called after Robert Emmet is in curious juxtaposition to that which takes its name from John Fitzgibbon[57], Earl of Clare, his contemporary; for the two were wide as the poles asunder in politics. North Summer Street (1809) is called Moor Street in old maps. No. 9 North Summer Street was the residence over a hundred years ago of the Hon. Mrs. Whitehead, a sister of the first Lord Ffrench, and the home in boyhood of her son, the Rev. Dr. Whitehead, afterwards Vice-President of Maynooth College.

Rutland and Buckingham Street both date from the last decade of the eighteenth century, and take their names from Viceroys of a few years earlier. 36 Upper Buckingham Street was the residence of John O'Donovan, the eminent Irish scholar, and of his adventurous son Edmond, a pupil of Belvedere, afterwards famous for his daring journey to Merv[58]. The last six houses of Summer Hill are called Duke Row, and are perhaps named, like the adjoining Portland Row, from the third Duke of Portland who was Prime Minister 1807-9. Until a few years ago the eastern side of Portland Row was called Caroline Row. The name dates from 1795, being the year of the marriage of the lady who wished afterwards to have inscribed on her tomb 'Caroline of Brunswick, the injured Queen of England'. Great Brunswick Street was named at the same time. The little chapel of St. Joseph, built in 1853, and served by the saintly Father Henry Young until his death in 1869, and the charitable institution adjoining were founded in 1836 by Dr. Blake, afterwards Bishop of Dromore, and James Murphy, a pious layman who died, almost a centenarian, about twenty-five years ago. Meredyth Place, renamed Empress Place over twenty years ago, dates from 1798. North William Street and Clarence Street, both a little over a century old, are evidently called after William, Duke of Clarence, afterwards William IV. Watty Cox, editor of the *Irish Magazine,* a celebrated political character of a century ago, lived at a house called Cox's Cot in North Clarence Street.

The convent in North William Street was about one hundred and ten years ago tenanted by Mrs. Aikenhead and the pioneers of the Irish Sisters of Charity. It was then for many years a Carmelite Convent until the sisters removed to Hampton House, Drumcondra. Since 1857 it has been occupied by the French *Filles de Charité* of St. Vincent de Paul. The Convent Chapel was used from the first, like St. Joseph's, Portland Row, as a Chapel of Ease for the Cathedral parish. In 1867 the district bounded by Drumcondra Road, the North Circular Road, the North Strand, and the Tolka was erected into a separate parish and this was the parish church. It had been separately administered for a long time previously, and the church and parish were named after St. Agatha, the Sicilian virgin and martyr, by Cardinal Cullen, who had passed the most of his life in the Irish College, Rome, which adjoins the Church of its patroness, Sant' Agata dei Goti. New St. Agatha's Church in North William Street was opened oh the 25th of October, 1908.

The Ordnance Survey map marks the 'Osiers' on the Royal Canal bank at the end of North Richmond Street, but the willows have long since disappeared. Clarke's Bridge, by which this ancient thoroughfare crosses the Royal Canal, is called after Edward Clarke, a director of the Canal Company in 1791 when the bridge was built. Long before the time of the Canal the old maps mark a solitary building, the only house on the road for a very long distance, called 'The Redd House' a name often given to a house built of red brick, then an unusual material. It stood near the site of Clarke's Bridge. On the western side of Ballybough Road and extending towards Clonliffe and Jones's Roads lies a townland with the singular name of Lovescharity, spelled thus in one word in the Ordnance maps and Townland Survey book. Love's Charity and Love Lane adjoining are apparently named from somebody surnamed Love. Smithborough[59] is now called Love Lane, while old Love Lane is now Sackville Avenue.

The last name and that of Sackville Garden, whose name-plate bears the date 1815, are evidently derived from the Rev. Sackville Ussher Lee, a clergyman residing at Exeter, who was an owner of property here. Up to a few years ago the first six houses of Ballybough Road were called Edward Terrace. They date from about 1815, and the name probably came from Edward, Duke of Kent, son of George III, and father of Queen Victoria. From him the late King Edward received his name. The next piece of the road was Foster Street, called, like Oriel Street not far off, from John Foster, afterwards Lords Oriel, the last Speaker of the Irish House of Commons. Charlemont Parade is called after his fellow-patriot who lived at Marino. Charleville Avenue, formerly Bay view Parade, and Charleville Mall seem to have some association with the family of Bury, Earls of Charleville, a title which became extinct in 1875.

Spring Garden Parade and Street, besides challenging an obvious comparison with Summer Hill, are called after an old 'tea-garden', a place of recreation long obsolete both here and in London, where there was also a Spring Garden. The name Mud Island, often popularly bestowed still on the district lying beside this part of Ballybough Road, is to be found in Cooke's Map of Dublin, 1821. It was a recognized place and even had its own king, but there is no ground for asserting that King's Lane, now Avenue, was the royal residence. That is said to have been situated about ninety years ago in Bayview Parade, now Charleville Avenue. The name of Carey's Lane here was changed in 1883, when an individual of that name became prominent by turning Queen's evidence; and in the same year the name of Brady's Row, off Mount joy Street, was abandoned, as that was the surname of the best known member of the Invincibles, who was executed. Poplar Row has been sometimes called Sandy Row of late. The name suggests the 12th of July in Belfast. Here is Taaffe's Place and the Ordnance Map marks a district here with the odd name, for a city locality, of Taaffe's Village from the owners of the property. Hackett's Buildings, at a point on the North Strand Road where Baths (sea) are marked over a century ago, were also called from the former proprietors who lived first here and afterwards in Amiens Street.

CHAPTER X

Between The Old and The New Roads

to The Sea

A FTER THE OLD ROAD TO Ballybough Bridge the next district of the north city is that between Marl-borough Street and Amiens Street, and the present road thence from the city, by the North Strand, to Clontarf and the sea. Eden Quay was called the Iron Quay a hundred and seventy years ago. It derives its present name from William Eden, first Lord Auckland, who had been Chief Secretary some fourteen years before the quay received its new name in 1796. In a letter written by him in 1782 he requests that his name may be bestowed on some new street, 'If our great plans should ever go into execution for the improvement of Dublin'. The letter is addressed to the Right Hon. John Beresford, a member of the great family, who lived in Marlborough Street, and a man who wielded immense political power. Whatever objections may be urged against his use of this, it cannot be denied that he effected much in the adornment of this city. He was Chief Commissioner of the Revenue for twenty-two most fateful years of the history of Ireland, from 1780 to 1802. To him we owe the Custom House, built in 1701 by James Lever, the father of the novelist[60]. The fine crescent called Beresford Place was named after him.

Northumberland Buildings at the end of the quay, and Northumberland Square adjoining, are called after Hugh Percy, Duke of Northumberland, Lord Lieutenant 1829-30, who is described as very wealthy and generous. The hotel at the corner bears the inscription, 'Northumberland Chop House, 1829'. Chop houses were then common in Dublin and London. A ship's instrument shop on Eden Quay bore for many years, until about two years ago, an effigy of a little wooden mid-shipman, in imitation of such a shop and such an effigy in Dickens's[61] *Dombey and Son,* some scenes of which are laid in a quarter of London corresponding to this Port district of Dublin. Another memorial of the story was Florence Place, apparently called after the heroine. It was on the East Wall, between Mayor Street and the North Wall, and disappeared in 1875, the houses being demolished when the Great Southern Railway Station was built, thus suffering the fate of a locality in the story.

Marlborough Street is called on the older maps Great Marlborough Street from the great Duke of Marlborough, from whose time it dates. The projected neighbouring Blenheim Street was called after his 'glorious victory'. Tyrone House in Marlborough Street, which has been the Office of the Commissioners of National Education since 1835[62], was built for the Beresford family, Earls of Tyrone, by Richard Cassells in 1741, being the first stone private house erected in Dublin. The ancient Irish county name which it bears was conferred in 1886 on the adjoining Upper Mecklenburgh Street, which joins Marlborough Street with Lower Gardiner Street. About three years afterwards the name was also appropriated by the longer and more eastern Lower Mecklenburgh Street. Similarly the eastern end of Lower Gloucester Street, between Buckingham Street and the North Strand, has been renamed Killarney Street, but no appropriation of this name by the rest of Gloucester Street has taken place as yet.

Great Martin's Lane was in 1765 named Mecklenburgh Street from Princess Charlotte of Mecklenburgh who had been married four years earlier to George III. Up to about ninety years ago physicians, barristers and attorneys resided in this street. The Misses Gunning, so celebrated in the eighteenth century, of whom one became Countess of Coventry and another Duchess of Hamilton and afterwards Duchess of Argyll, were born at their father's residence in this street. As already mentioned the Botanic Garden of the Royal Dublin Society was at Great Martin's Lane or Mecklenburgh Street from 1735 until 1795, when it was transferred to its present position in Glasnevin.

Little Martin's Lane was in 1811 named Beaver Street. Palace Yard near this was not so magnificent as the name would seem to imply. Uxbridge in this district is called after the Marquess of Anglesey who was Lord Lieutenant 1828-9 and 1830-3. He was also Earl of Uxbridge, and under this title was distinguished in the Waterloo campaign where he lost a leg.

The aristocratic character of the neighbourhood in the eighteenth century may be conjectured from its containing the fine residence of the Beresford family. In those days Great Marlborough Street ended at the corner of Lower Abbey Street, then called Ship Buildings. There was a narrow lane to the riverside called Ferryboat Lane or Union Lane a hundred and seventy years ago. When this lane was widened the new short street to Eden Quay was for some years after 1776 called Union Street before it became merged in Marlborough Street. In the old days of Great Marlborough Street a large house stood at its junction with Abbey Street, the residence of George Felster, a wealthy merchant.

The Earl of Tyrone was in 1789 created Marquess of Waterford and the house is called Waterford House on maps after that year, but the original name seems to have held its ground. The ghostly legend embodied by Sir Walter Scott in his impressive poem, *The Eve of St. John,* was borrowed, as he acknowledges, from a ghost story told of Lady Beresford and the Earl of Tyrone[63].

Marlborough Bowling Green, a fashionable place of resort from the middle of the eighteenth century, was situated in the block formed by Marlborough Street, Talbot Street, Gardiner Street and Abbey Street. This once interesting block contained other noteworthy places long gone. There is an old novel which first appeared in 1798 and which is still published and read, the *Children of the Abbey,* by Mrs. Regina Roche, a Waterford lady. In this picture of eighteenth-century Irish fashionable life joined to an ultra-sentimental melodrama now laughable, Capel Street appears as the fashionable promenade of Dublin, and Marlborough Green is visited as a matter of course. Marlborough Green is said to have received its death-blow as a fashionable resort from an unfortunate occurrence in 1761. Lord Westmeath's son and heir was killed in a duel by Captain O'Reilly, and the quarrel began in Marlborough Green.

The projected Blenheim Street was also in this block. It appears in maps and directories in the end of the eighteenth century and disappears in the thirties of the nineteenth. It was to have run from 86 Talbot Street, now the Belfast Bank. The house demolished to make way for it bore the inscription 'Carolin's Buildings, 1810', that old Dublin mercantile family having built many houses in this district. Blenheim Street was to have joined Talbot Street to Abbey Street, and the southern portion of it was transformed into

Northumberland Square in 1844. Much of the site of Blenheim Street with other places adjoining, like the Jewish Synagogue of 1746 in Marlborough Green, the Velvet Manufactory of over a century ago near Trinity Church, and Pugh's Glass Factory in Potter's Alley, has been absorbed by the large premises of Brooks, Thomas and Co.

The street now called Talbot Street dates also from the end of the eighteenth century. It appears on maps in 1800 as (North) Cope Street, but this name was probably applied to the western end, for the name 'Moland Street 1810' was to be found, until the name Talbot Street was recently unnecessarily painted over it, on an old name-plate on the house at the corner of Talbot Street and Gardiner Street, the corner of the Marlborough Green block. The date on the name-plate was 1810, and in Campbell's Map of Dublin, 1811, the eastern half of Talbot Street appears as Moland Street, the western being marked Cope Street. The present Talbot Street thoroughfare terminated then at the corner of Mabbot Street. The portion to Amiens Street had not yet been made. The name Moland Street in older maps and directories, beginning with 1795 is applied to another projected street in this Marlborough Green block.

This other projected Moland Street stretches, on the maps, from the projected Blenheim Street eastwards to the foot of Mabbot Street, including the present Beresford Lane and Frenchman's Lane. The latter name is found in Rocque's Map of Dublin, 1756. The same map marks Cezar's Lane, long since vanished, off Frenchman's Lane. An extinct street called Lime Street is on this map. It ran from Frenchman's Lane to what is now Beresford Place (The Strand) parallel to the present Lower Gardiner Street. Moland Street or Cope Street was renamed Talbot Street in 1821 after Charles, Earl Talbot, who was then Lord Lieutenant. The name Moland is that of a family who are returned in Valuation Office blue-books of eighty years ago conjointly with a family named Deverell, as owners of property in the district. Hence the name of Deverell Place off Lower Gardiner Street, the rere entrance to the premises of the Commissioners of National Education. Moland Place, dating from 1840, preserves the name. It is beside the Welsh Church, erected in 1838. Many of the small Welsh colony in Dublin have always resided in this district.

This neighbourhood must ever remain associated with the name of Charles Lever. He was born at 35 Amiens[64] Street, demolished over twenty years ago to make way for the Loop Line Railway. The house was the residence of his father, James Lever, an Englishman, an architect and builder employed on the adjoining new Custom House. James Lever assisted also in the erection of St. Patrick's College, Maynooth, and was on friendly terms with some of the first professors. The novelist was born in Amiens Street on the 1st of September, 1806. The late Dr. W. J. Fitzpatrick is in error when he states, in his *Life of Lever,* that Amiens Street received its name from the Peace of Amiens concluded in 1802. The name is found in 1800 and is derived from the title Viscount Amiens, a minor title of the Earl of Aldborough, who built Aldborough House close by.

Charles Lever lived afterwards and practised as a young physician in another house built by his father and still standing. It is now numbered 67 Talbot Street. He also passed much of his boyhood in a third house built by his father, Moatfield, just outside the village of Coolock, where there is a moat on the lawn. Fitzpatrick describes Moatfield as situated in the Green Lanes of Clontarf, from which it is quite a long way off. The Green Lanes are introduced, however, into *That Boy of Norton's.* James Lever built and owned other houses in Mabbot Street and Montgomery Street, and left them to his two sons, Charles and the Rev. John Lever, who was the senior of the novelist by ten years. The deterioration of this property began in Charles Lever's lifetime and caused him much annoyance. Spencer's Row, off Talbot Street, is apparently called after that John Spencer who was Charles Lever's early friend and correspondent.

The southern portion of Lower Gardiner Street appears in Rocque's Map, 1756, as The Old Rope Walk. Mabbot Street, parallel to it, is much older. It is called after Gilbert Mabbot, who erected a watermill here before 1674. It must be remembered that this was then the seashore, and a map of this coast in 1717 marks a 'corner of Mabbot Wall', once the sea-wall. Mabbot's mill, mill-pond and land extended back from the present Talbot Street to the road which is now Montgomery Street. This picturesque idea of the antecedents of Mabbot Street, is even surpassed by that of Montgomery Street, which was such a remote and rural district to the citizens of Dublin, that it was called World's End Lane. An elder daughter of Sir William Montgomery, Bart., married Luke Gardiner, Lord Mountjoy; but a younger, from whom this street was named Montgomery Street in 1776, married John Beresford who was so active in developing this district. It was greatly improved about twenty years ago and renamed Foley Street after the great sculptor, who was born in No. 6 Montgomery Street in 1818[65].

Cumberland Street dates from 1766 and Gloucester Street from about ten years later. The first is from the Duke of Cumberland, son of George II, stingingly referred to in Thackeray's *Virginians* as the Duke of Culloden and Fontenoy. The second is from the Duke of Gloucester, brother of George III. The houses in both, and especially in Upper Gloucester Street, are very fine. In the latter street two great Irish judicial dignitaries, one of whom was a peer, were born in 1837 at Nos. 5 and 29. Lady Anne's Lane is off Cumberland Street. Gloucester Diamond and Gloucester Terrace in Gloucester Street are architectural embellishments of this once fine street. The Church of Our Lady of Lourdes has been founded in this congested district. The toy street off it, called Mulgrave Place, bears date 1835, when the popular Earl of Mulgrave (Marquess of Normanby) was Viceroy. In the first half of the last century the Kane family resided in Gloucester Street. They were manufacturing chemists with an extensive concern on the North Wall. Sir Robert Kane, author of *The Industrial Resources of Ireland,* made many discoveries in chemistry. His son, Captain, since then Admiral Kane, became famous for his rescue, by skilful seamanship, of his ship the *Calliope* in the great hurricane at Samoa on the 16th of March, 1889, when all the other warships present—three German and three American, perished. Many other members of the Kane family, some still living, have been distinguished in various walks of life.

CHAPTER XI

THE NEW ROAD TO THE SEA

STARTING FROM THE CUSTOM HOUSE, the new road to the sea runs by Store Street, Amiens Street and the North Strand, and, crossing Annesley Bridge, reaches Clontarf. Store Street is named after the Custom House stores, erected about 1791. There was a building here, where Mabbot Street joins Store Street, marked 'China Manafactuary'. The map-makers of the eighteenth century were no purists in orthography. The maps made after the embankment of the quays at the North Wall in 1717, but before the building of the Custom House in 1791 (which stands on what was called Amory's Ground), mark the whole thoroughfare 'Strand' from the present North Strand to as far west as Beresford Place. One old map marks it 'The Street'. The name Amiens Street supplanted the name Strand in 1800, but it appears then to have been applied, perhaps in error, to that eastern end of Gloucester Street which has recently been dubbed Killarney Street. But it was certainly applied to the present street before the birth of Charles Lever in 1806. So rural an institution as a Pound stood on the site of the present Amiens Street Terminus a hundred and seventy years ago. The North Strand first bears the prefix North in 1803. With Talbot Street and Amiens Street it has, since the construction of Annesley Bridge in 1797, quite superseded Summer Hill and Ballybough Road as the road to the sea, Clontarf, Howth, Malahide, Artane, Coolock, Raheny, Dolly-mount, Baldoyle, Portmarnock, and generally to that important, picturesque and rapidly improving coast and inland district lying to the north-east of Dublin, of which the ever-beautiful Howth is the chief ornament.

Preston Street, the short street off Amiens Street, dates from 1817. This street ran to the West Road (the present Oriel Street) before the Railway was made. So did another unnamed street from Amiens Street. A street here, called Hart Street, of about the same date, has long disappeared. It is now represented by the street called Railway Arches, which was formerly included in Sheriff Street. The name of Inkerman Cottages indicates the date. Nixon's Buildings, and Nixon Street not far off, are named from owners of property. Newcomen Bridge, by which the North Strand crosses the Royal Canal, is called after Sir William Gleadowe Newcomen, Bart., one of the Directors of the Canal Company in 1791. Another Director at that time was the Hon. Richard Annesley; but it is probable that Annesley Bridge, by which the North Strand crosses the mouth of the Tolka, and used to touch until recently the innermost corner of Dublin Bay, is not called after him. Annesley Bridge was perhaps named in compliment to the first Lord Annesley and Viscount Glerawley, who was married to a sister of the powerful John Beresford, Commissioner of Revenue, who had so much to do with the development of north-east Dublin. It will be remembered that Annesley House, on the site of the present Pro-Cathedral, stood in Marlborough Street, opposite to Tyrone House, the residence of Lady Annesley's father and brother.

Off the North Strand is Xavier Avenue, whose name tells its origin. Opposite to it is Waterloo Avenue, another historic memorial. Nottingham Street, a name as old as 1798, had until a few years ago a large house at the corner which must have dated from that year. Ninety years ago there was a street called Noy Street near the North Strand. Like Philip Street (Summer Hill), and Booker's Row (Custom House), its very site cannot now be found. Hoey's Avenue, so named fifty years ago, was changed after a few years to Strandville Avenue. The new name is rather inconvenient as there is another and older Strandville Avenue in Clontarf at no great distance from the new[66]. But Bayview Avenue (called after Bayview on the North Strand) which dates from the earlier thirties, was made a complete misnomer a few years after it was built ; for the newly-constructed Great Northern Railway shut out altogether the view of the sea. The French spelling Bévue would now be more appropriate.

Aldborough House, the most considerable building in this district, fronts Portland Row and stands at the junction of that street with the North Strand, Amiens Street, Gloucester Street and Seville Place. The house and grounds form a complete and extensive block or square, fronting Portland Row, Gloucester Street, Buckingham Street, and Meredyth Place. In the roadway here, where a turnpike stood over a hundred years ago, is an ornamental drinking fountain erected to the memory of the late General Henry Hall. C.B., of the Indian Army, a resident of Co. Galway, Aldborough House was built in 1796 by Edward Stratford, second Earl of Aldborough and Viscount Amiens, from whom Aldborough Place, Amiens Street and Stratford Row receive their names[67]. At that time the North Strand had just become a very important avenue of communication between the city and Howth and Clontarf, owing to the making of the new (Annesley) Bridge over the mouth of the Tolka. Aldborough House, one of the grandest of the Dublin residences of the eighteenth-century nobility, was erected at a cost of £40,000, and was so splendidly complete, that it contained even a theatre[68]. Aldborough House, Dublin, soon passed out of the hands of this family and has had a chequered history since. Shortly after the Stratfords had sold it, it became a Feinaglian School, to which Clonliffe House was an auxiliary. Aldborough House was conducted by Von Feinagle, whose system of education, relying principally on the exercise of the memory, had then a great vogue in Dublin. Feinagle died here in 1819. In maps of Dublin, dated in his time and for long afterwards the great house is marked 'Luxemburgh', of which Grand Duchy Feinagle was a native. It was afterwards a military barrack, being the headquarters of the Commissariat Department, and is now a branch of the General Post Office. That department of the public service is to be commended for the care it has shewn itself prepared to take of this fine old structure and its surroundings.

CHAPTER XII

THE NORTH WALL AND THE NORTH LOTTS

C USTOM HOUSE QUAY DATES FROM 1791 when the new Custom House was built[69]. The North Wall Slip was on the quay, a little to the east of the late Old Dock gate. The Old Dock is now filled up. George's Dock, called after George IV, was opened by that sovereign in 1821, and the Inner, or Revenue Dock, the larger of the two, dates from the same time. From this point we are in the district of the Dublin Port and Docks Board, more anciently the Ballast Board, and the peculiar uniform of the Quay Police, who arc its officials, is to be seen from this to the 'Point of the Wall'. The King's Excise Store in Mayor Street was also opened in 1821. Five ferries ply between the North Wall and the southern bank of the river.

There is a long row of stores, sheds and wharves here belonging to steampacket companies. All the great Irish railway companies have stations at the North Wall, for almost all the passenger traffic and much of the goods traffic of the Port of Dublin is carried on there. The garden of the London and North Western Railway Company's Hotel is a green oasis in this desert. The Harbour Master's garden is another. The North Wall Extension, dating from 1875, and since enlarged, contains berthage for the biggest fourmasters; also the new and fine Alexandra Basin, called after the late Queen, which could hold all the old Docks; and, best of all, for Dublin, the prosperous ship-building yard of the Dublin Dockyard Company, established over twenty years ago, by Messrs. Walter Scott and Smillie, and doing more work every day. The Graving Dock, Customs Watch House and Hundred Ton Crane are also features of the Extension. The road beside the Great Southern Station, once the extreme eastern limit of Dublin, is marked on old maps as containing Shalloway's Baths and Halpin's Pond, while the neighbouring sandbank was called Brown's Patch. These places have disappeared with the march of improvement in the Port of Dublin.

The embankment of the Liffey at this point, begun in 1717, was completed in 1729 by the erection of the North Wall. That large portion of Dublin bounded by the North Wall, East Wall, North Strand and Amiens Street was reclaimed from the sea about that time. It includes the greater portion of the North Dock Ward and of the Catholic parish of St. Laurence O'Toole. It is called the North Lotts because the Corporation in 1717 drew lots for the distribution amongst themselves of the land to be acquired here by the construction of the North Wall. They also shared the land amongst themselves in portions called lots. There were dry lots and wet lots, as may be seen by inspection of the curious old map on which this district is divided into squares, each containing the name of the fortunate grantee. The dry lots are those which were in fact reclaimed. The wet lots are those which, though marked on the map as granted, still remain covered by the tide. But the proprietorial rights of the grantees in the latter have always remained; and some years ago the Corporation granted compensation to a Dublin gentleman, the direct descendant of the original grantee, who owned a wet lot inside the Northern Railway in the space now reclaimed.

The North Lotts district is sometimes humorously called Newfoundland on account of its having being reclaimed from the sea, and there is actually a Newfoundland Street within its limits. On the exact spot where Newfoundland Street and Nixon Street are now built, Campbell's Map of Dublin, 1811, marks an 'Intended Floating Dock', never constructed. The Corporation also honoured itself by conferring on the new streets laid out here the names of Mayor Street, Sheriff Street, Guild Street and Commons Street, after the Lord Mayor, the Sheriffs, the Guilds of each trade of which the Corporation was then composed, and the Commons who elected them. Wapping Street is reminiscent of the kindred London dock district sung in *Wapping Old Stairs*. Fish Street is apparently a recollection of the street of the same name near London Bridge[70].

Seville Place, a long section of the North Circular Road[71], seems to derive its name from the capture of Seville by the British in the Peninsular War in

1812. Oriel Street is from Lord Oriel (Speaker Foster), Canning Place, beside Jane Place, is perhaps from the great statesman, George Canning. Whitworth Row (1821) is from Charles, Earl Whitworth[72], and Coburgh Place (1822), like Coburgh Gardens, opened in 1817, and now the beautiful and extensive pleasure-ground at the rere of Lord Iveagh's house in Stephen's Green, takes its name from the family of Saxe Coburgh to which both the mother and the husband of Queen Victoria belonged[73]. Coburgh Place was always a separate thoroughfare from Seville Lane, even before the railway was made. The Church of St. Laurence O'Toole was completed in 1853[74], and this district was formed into a new parish, having previously belonged to the Cathedral parish. The Spencer Dock, where Sheriff Street crosses the Royal Canal, was opened by Earl Spencer, Lord Lieutenant, on the 15th of April, 1873.

It is easy to understand the names of the East Road, and the West Road, but the origin of that of Church Road (to which the definite article is usually prefixed by the people of the district) is very singular. St. Laurence O'Toole's Church was built in 1853, the Protestant Church of St. Barnabas close by in 1870. There was no church in the neighbourhood when the road was first named Church Road early in the eighteenth century. But the road was called after a church which it was intended should be built here, an intention since fulfilled[75]. This is clear from inspection of a very strange old map of this part of Dublin, made for the Corporation in 1717, which marks as existing a great number of other roads and places, some destined never to be reclaimed from the sea, others on existing dry land like 'the Church Road'. On this map we find Market Road called after a Market which, like the Church, never took shape save in the imagination of those who made the map. On a spot still covered by the tide, as it was over two hundred years ago, when the map was drawn, we find Island Road and Island Quay, to be called after the adjacent Island of Clontarf[76].

But it is satisfactory to note that the projectors, however, extensive their plans for reclamation from the sea, did not contemplate that abolition of the Island, a place with a history, which has unfortunately been effected in our own days.

The West Road was much more extensive in older times than it is now. It ran from the seashore to the junction of Sheriff Street with Commons Street. The construction of the Royal Canal cut it in two and the southern half received its present name of Oriel Street. That Oriel Street and the West Road were once a single thoroughfare may appear somewhat surprising to those who know the district now, but the truth of the fact will be at once evident to anybody who looks across the Royal Canal at this point from either side. No road in this part of Dublin, and that is saying much, has suffered as much demolition as the northern half of the old West Road. The fruitful source of such demolition in the North Lotts or 'Newfoundland' is the making of new lines of railway. At present the West Road starts from the seashore at the eastern side of the Great Northern Railway. West of the railway line is Stoney Road, misspelled Stony on the Ordnance Survey Map, called after Dr. Bindon Stoney, Engineer to the Port and Docks Board, who carried out the Extension and Basin at the North Wall on so grand a scale. About half way between the sea and the canal the West Road is suddenly transformed by the junction of several railways into a hopeless chaos of ways (some of which are no thoroughfares) which confronts the bewildered traveller. By patient study the explorer discovers that there are only two outlets, one through Ossory Road, leading to Newcomen Bridge and the North Strand, and another by Hawthorne Terrace to Church Road.

The fate of absorption by railways, already mentioned as assigned to a London district in one of Dickens's stories, has also befallen the southern end of Church Road. This road once joined Seville Place at the corner opposite to St. Laurence O'Toole's Church. First the Canal effected a slight severance more than a century ago. Then came the railways, and Blythe's Avenue, dated 1863, has acquired a peculiar air of detachment, and, although it is well inland, the ships in the Spencer Dock seem to form a part of it. The same remark applies to the end of Lower Oriel Street. Anybody who walks up Church Road from the sea with the intention of reaching Spencer Dock will find himself compelled to make a considerable detour, with some climbing, into the East Road. The last road, being the shortest and most easterly of the three, East, Church and West, has held its own best in the desperate struggle for existence of the thoroughfares in this neighbourhood. Another desolate no-thoroughfare is East Mayor Street, which once ran to the East Wall beside the long-lost Florence Place. It is now like Ulubræ in Horace 'the back of God speed' in Anglo-Irish. It is Tadmor in the wilderness or the desolation of Balclutha in Ossian.

The most interesting building in this district was Castle Forbes, Upper Sheriff Street. It was a tall old house, standing as directly on the street as

Hawthorne's *House of the Seven Gables* which it recalled in many ways. The stone containing the inscription 'Castle Forbes, 1729', in the curling letters and numerals of the eighteenth century, is at some distance from the house. If that date referred to the late building, Castle Forbes was probably the oldest house on the north side of Dublin, and was surpassed in age by only a very few years by any old house on the south side, of which there are still some in the Liberties. Old maps of this district of North Lotts mark another old house called Forbes Castle (in ruins) on the East Road; to which perhaps the date on the stone is equally applicable; also the martially sounding names of Fort William in Upper Sheriff Street and Fort Crystal, a very handsome building long vanished, where Church Road meets the sea. There are still Fort Lodge on the West Road, and Fort Crystal Terrace. Northcourt Avenue, Lower Middle and Upper, off Church Road, misspelled Northcote Avenue on some maps, was formerly called North's Court from a house here.

But only Castle Forbes remained, and it was probably the oldest, for the date is about the earliest at which a house could have been built here, although the late building scarcely looked as much as a hundred and eighty years old. It looked much taller, viewed from the side, than from the front. The door in Sheriff Street was modern, the old front door being on the side remote from the street. The house must have been very conspicuous when it was the only building in this district, as it was for many years. Lately it was surrounded by buildings and chimneys, but was still remarkable for its ancient and quaint aspect. It was evidently built by some one called Forbes. We find members of that Highland clan in Dublin a long time ago. Perhaps the builder of this relic of the early days of the Hanoverian succession was George Forbes, who was Lord Mayor in 1720. It was afterwards for many years the residence of the Carolin family who have been long connected with the commerce of Dublin. Some years ago it was the office of a glass bottle company, whose works adjoined it. It was lastly in possession of Messrs. Martin, whose name has been honourably identified with the Port of Dublin for more than a century. Though a little the worse for wear it was in pretty good preservation[77].

The East Wall which bounds this district of North Lotts runs along the seashore from Annesley Bridge, North Strand to the extremity of the North Wall. From its eastern angle a fine view of Clontarf, Howth and the northern portion of the Bay is obtained. The East Wall is sometimes called the Wharf

Road from the Wharf, a slip apparently constructed more than a century ago for the use of bathers and still so used. There is a stone platform here used by divers called from its form the Smoothing Iron. The great depth of water is secured by the Tolka current which runs between the mainland and Clontarf Island.

CHAPTER XIII

CLONTARF ISLAND

IT IS HARD TO REALIZE now, when three or four miles of land occupy a space where once the sea flowed, what an important and conspicuous object in Dublin Bay Clontarf Island was. The name may seem a misnomer now that the Dublin City mainland has been brought, since two hundred and twenty years ago to within a short distance of the island, but it should be borne in mind that, before that time, Clontarf was the nearest point of the shore to this island, which, to this day, has always formed a portion of the Clontarf estate. Before the North Lotts became dry land, the Island lay far out to sea from any point of the mainland, when the coast line ran from Ballybough Bridge by Amiens Street, Beresford Place and Strand Street to the site of Essex Bridge. This may easily be verified by looking at the interesting map of Dublin in 1673 in Haliday's *History of the Scandinavian Kingdom of Dublin.* The old wide harbour of Dublin contained no more prominent landmark than the Island.

Such a place, set in the deep water of the Tolka current where it joined the greater Liffey current, must have been a splendid point of vantage in the Battle of Clontarf, which, we arc assured by the best historians, raged most fiercely around the mouth of the Tolka. The sea forces of the Danes might find the Island a convenience. In 1538 the Prior of Kilmainham granted a lease of Clontarf, naming also this Island, to Matthew King. Although the Island, with the rest of the Clontarf possessions of Kilmainham Priory, was granted in 1600 to Sir Geoffrey Fenton and in 1608 to his son William, the King family continued in possession; for Carte's *Life of Ormonde* states, that

Sir Charles Coote in 1641 burned most of Clontarf town, especially Mr. George King's house. Mr. King, having adhered to the cause of Charles I, was attainted, and his estates, comprising, we are told, 'this manor' (of Clontarf), 'Hollybrooks and the Island of Clontarf', were granted to John Blackwell, a favourite of Cromwell, who assigned his interest to John Vernon, whose descendants still possess the estate.

We find an apparently contradictory account in the *Parliamentary Gazetteer of Ireland,* published eighty years ago. It is there stated that Clontarf Island was granted to a certain Captain Cromwell, a kinsman of Oliver, on its forfeiture by Mr. George King. It is an odd coincidence that the Island was occupied in modern times by a man named Christopher Cromwell, as a tenant of the Vernon family. The Island is often called Cromwell's Island by old Dublin citizens after this latter-day Cromwell, who was a publican in Beaver Street, where Cromwell's Court still recalls his memory.

Christopher Cromwell built a wooden house on the Island at a cost of £45 and often stayed there for a week at a time, using it in fact as a kind of summer residence. This habit of his had a tragic ending. On the night of the 9th of October, 1844, the greatest storm recorded in the annals of the Port of Dublin raged. The cellars on the North Wall were flooded. The sea encroached once more on the extensive tract which had once lain under it. The road on the East Wall was impassable, and the waves washed over the roof of the Wharf Tavern, an old house still standing where the East Road meets the sea. The constable on duty, whose beat lay under the water, watching from the nearest safe point, saw the light go out in Cromwell's wooden house on the Island at ten o'clock. Next day when the storm subsided, the bodies of Cromwell and his son William, a boy of ten, were found on the Island shore. The bodies had been retained there by the heavy fishing boots which they wore. But the boats had been carried as far as Annesley Bridge; while the wooden house, demolished by the storm, had been dashed against the embankment of the Great Northern Railway where it crosses the sea. This embankment had been made only in the preceding year by Sir John McNeill, whose 'Skew Bridge', where the Railway crosses the sea road at Clontarf, was then regarded as a triumph of engineering. Thus the line endured its worst trial when only just made.

Whatever may be the authority for asserting that Clontarf Island was granted to Captain Cromwell, there is no doubt that it has belonged, as well as the remainder of the Clontarf estate, to the Vernon family since the days of Oliver. John Vernon, the first possessor, was a younger son of an ancient and noble English family. One of these Vernons had acquired by marriage the property of the family of 'Peveril of the Peak', descended from William the Conqueror. It is probable that Glendinning's marriage to the heiress of Avenel in Scott's *Abbot* is founded on the circumstance of the marriage of a Vernon with the heiress of Avenel, by which Haddon in Derbyshire was acquired by the Vernons. Sir George Vernon of Haddon in the sixteenth century was, on account of his great wealth, called 'the King of the Peak'. His daughter Dorothy married Sir John Manners, ancestor of the Duke of Rutland. The romantic circumstances of this marriage are commemorated in Haddon Hall. This historic Derbyshire estate of Haddon received a memorial over thirty years ago in the newly-built Haddon Road adjoining Clontarf Castle. The first holder of the title of Lord Vernon, created in 1762, and still existing, was a great-grand-nephew of John Vernon, the first of the name in Clontarf Castle and Island. This John being, as has been said, a Cromwellian was Quartermaster-General of the Army in Ireland. His son and successor, Colonel Edward Vernon, who bore the same name and title as the late owner, is said, unlike his father, to have served the Stuarts. He was a Cavalier, who fought for Kings Charles the First and Second, both in England and Ireland.

In 1695 John Vernon, cousin of the Colonel, claimed the property from the latter and succeeded. In John Vernon's petition to the Irish Parliament he claims amongst other property, 'the Islands'. The word is in the plural, as in the grant of 1608, evidently because the North Bull, then very small, and only about a century old in its present extent (a portion of which was also a part of the Vernon estate, but now belongs to the Most Rev, the Hon. B. J. Plunket), is practically an island but for the bridge and Bull Wall, which are of comparatively modern construction.

Some twenty years later there was much controversy and litigation between the Vernon family and the Corporation of Dublin concerning a tract of strand referred to by the Vernons as 'the Pool and Island of Clontarf'. The Corporation claimed that it was within their franchises and was their property. But Captain John Vernon in a speech made in 1731, which was printed by George Faulkner, stoutly asserted his right to the Island and reminded the Corporation that the liberties of the city on the north were bounded, according to their charter *de libertatibus* of the second of King

John, 'by the lands of Clonliffe, by the Tolka, and by the Church of St. Mary, Oxmantown' (St. Mary's Abbey).

Whatever may have been the rights of this controversy it will be noted that this Vernon claim that the Island was outside the city boundary was made after the reclamation of the North Lotts, when the Island lay, as it still does, a few yards from the City shore. Clontarf Island has been marked on the Ordnance Maps for many years past as within the City Parliamentary and Municipal boundary; as Clontarf mainland certainly is for the last thirty-two years. The Island was of use to the City in 1650 when it was made an isolation place for those afflicted with the plague which then raged in Dublin.

Eighteenth-century maps show 'The Island' as a ribbon-shaped piece of land with one end facing the Wharf, and 'The Island House', apparently a more ambitious structure than the little wooden house many may remember. The Island House is described in a book on Dublin, published over a century ago, as a place of recreation for the citizens, and the Island as a conspicuous object on a journey by land to Howth. Maps of the Protestant parish of Clontarf still include the Island as a part of the parish. The Ordnance Survey Maps of Dublin, until a few years ago marked both the Island and. the Bathing Pond. A Valuation Blue Book of sixty years ago mentions the 'Bathing Island', of which Mr. Vernon is returned as landlord and Mrs. Toole as tenant. Many may remember the Bathing Island Ferry Barge, plying from the Wharf, and the Bathing Pond, where swimming with corks was practised.

But the Island has disappeared. This is the result of the continuous removal of its sands for manure at low tide. There is a notice of the Port and Docks Board at several points on the Clontarf Road, dated 5th of April, 1883, expressly prohibiting, under penalties, the removal of sand from 'the Island of Clontarf'. But this prohibition would seem to have applied to those only who neglected to pay; for at high tide all that is now visible of the Island is the top of a few posts or stakes, the ruins of the last wooden house. At low tide the outline may still be made out, as it is distinguished from the surrounding bed of the sea by its stony surface, and still slightly greater elevation. The Bathing Pond in the sands and the ruins of the slippery wooden causeway leading from the Ferry Barge's landing-stage to the Island House may also be discerned when the tide is out. It is a pity that no effort should have been made to preserve this spot of Old Dublin, which has a history; the more so since it is probable that there is a natural accumulation of sand at this point, which would, if not removed, once more form this little Island and perpetuate a place as old as any part of Ireland, when the three or four miles of the adjoining district of Dublin were but newly recovered from the sea.

CHAPTER XIV

FAIRVIEW AND MARINO

THE NAME FAIRVIEW SUPERSEDED THAT of Ballybough early in the nineteenth century. Passing beyond the old city boundary at Ballybough Bridge, one of the first objects of interest is the Catholic parish Church of Fairview, which is between seventy and eighty years old. The building which was its predecessor, previously a Dominican Convent, is on Fairview Strand, a little beyond Fairview Avenue. This parish corresponds mainly with the old parish of Clonturk, which takes its name from a townland on the high road to Swords. The balustrade in front of Clonturk House, Drumcondra, belonged to old Carlisle Bridge. Although the latter half of the word resembles the Irish *torc*, boar, the meaning of Clonturk is said to be 'plain of the Tolka', of which turk is a corruption.

Close by the Church is Philipsburgh Avenue, which perhaps derives its name from Philipsburg on the Rhine where the Duke of Berwick was killed in 1734. On old maps the name of this avenue is Ellis's Lane. It was the principal road of the suburb of Annadale, once chiefly inhabited by the Dublin Jewish colony. In many old houses here and on Richmond Road the door did not face the street directly, and this is said to have been a usage of the Jews of that time who had their Synagogue in Marlborough Green. There is a strange story of a Jewish tombstone in this district becoming the hearthstone of a Christian. The old Jewish burying ground, founded in 1718, is at Fairview, and on its little mortuary chapel the odd inscription confronts the passer-by: 'Built in the year 5618'. This date corresponds to the year of the

Christian era 1857-8, the Jewish year beginning on the 24th of September.

Croydon Park, at the end of Fairview Avenue, was, until about twenty years ago, the residence of the family of Staveley, connected with the County of Limerick, who lived here for over a century. Merville Avenue is a name a few years old for Big Gun, called after a tavern here, just as the Cross Guns at Glasnevin, formerly situated at the corner of the present Cemetery Avenue, have given name to a townland. Marino is reached immediately after. The piers of the grand gate designed by Cipriani bore the dragons of the Caulfeilds and their warlike motto, but the house built by Thomas Adderley and presented by him to his stepson, the Volunteer Earl of Charlemont, was quite thrown into the shade by the imposing new Novitiate of the Christian Brothers, erected in a commanding position on a height inland, and one of the most conspicuous buildings on the north side of Dublin. Some years ago the house was demolished and the Marino estate built upon. The Church of St. Vincent de Paul has been erected to supply this new district. The Caulfeild family left Marino in 1876, and the last Earl died in 1892, but the Viscounty passed to his cousin, the son of Edward Houston Caulfeild, the last Marshal of the Dublin Marshalsea. Marino Crescent, built in 1792, is said to have been built by one Ffolliott, a painter of Aungier Street, who, having some disagreement with Lord Charlemont, built this row of houses in order effectually to shut out the view of the sea from Marino House. Martin Haverty, the author of a painstaking and accurate History of Ireland, based on original documents, resided for many years at No. 21 Marino Crescent. He died on the 18th of January, 1887, at 40 St. Alphonsus Road, Drumcondra. In the fifties William Carleton, the Ulster novelist, lived at No. 3 Marino Terrace close by. He died in 1869 at No. 2 Woodville beside Milltown Park.

CHAPTER XV

THE MALAHIDE ROAD

MALAHIDE ROAD, WHICH IS SKIRTED by the wall of Marino, is one of the most cheerful highways near Dublin. Firstly, it passes in its course to Malahide through a continuous succession of villages. Donnycarney, Artane, Coolock, Balgriffin, St. Dolough's, Kinsaley and Feltrim succeed each other at short intervals. The road passes many pleasant country seats and richly-cultivated farms. In agriculture the North County Dublin is the most progressive district in Ireland. Besides this source of pleasure to the traveller the road is a typical centre of a prosperous inland scene, and yet is not too far from the coast.

Pleasant glimpses of the sea and the rocky shores of Howth and Ireland's Eye are caught. There are some unique views of the latter island from Malahide Road. In the grounds of the O'Brien Institute to the left of the road is the Temple or Casino designed by Sir William Chambers and erected by Lord Charlemont on a Grecian model. Both the building and its surroundings are eminently picturesque. The village of Donnycarney is next reached[78]. The road crosses the little stream called the Holly Brook, which flows through the grounds of Thorndale, by Scurlogue's Bridge, now Donnycarney Bridge, and into the sea at Strandville Avenue, Clontarf.

Beyond this bridge is the Artane Industrial School directed by the Christian Brothers. This splendid institution, founded in 1870, occupies the site of Artane Castle, long the property of the Hollywood family, one of whom was one of the most celebrated of the early Jesuits in Ireland, Father Christopher

Hollywood, or, as he is styled in Latin, Christophorus a Sacro Bosco. In 1534 Artane Castle was the scene of a historic tragedy. John Allen, Archbishop of Dublin, who owed his advancement to Cardinal Wolsey, shared his hostility to the Geraldines. When therefore in this year the rebellion of Silken Thomas broke out, Allen attempted to fly to England. He embarked, we are told, in 'the little haven at Dame Gate', near Dublin Castle which is very far west of any possible place of embarkation nowadays.[79] But the prelate's voyage was not destined to be long. He was stranded at Clontarf, whether through tempest or treachery is not clear. Had he sought his temporary refuge at Clontarf Island he would perhaps, have been safe, and might easily have embarked on another ship. But he went inland to the house of his friend Hollywood of Artane, where he was soon sought. On the next day, the 28th of July, he was dragged from the Castle and inhumanly murdered by the followers of Silken Thomas. The spot where this cruel deed was perpetrated was left neglected for centuries until some of the buildings of the Industrial School were erected on it[80]. Old Artane Castle was succeeded by the house, which is now the residence of the Christian Brothers, in 1825. This house was the residence for some time in his boyhood of the distinguished soldier and author, General Sir William Butler.

Nearly opposite the gate of Artane School is a narrow road called Killester Lane, traversing the old parish of that name, and leading to the Howth Road at the entrance of the once splendid residence of Killester House, where there is still a path called the Nuns' Walk. The Ordnance maps mark a building 'Convent in ruins' not far from this on the Howth Road. There is a modern house called Killester Abbey. The ruins of the old Church of Killester are in the churchyard adjoining Killester Lane. It was dedicated to St. Brigid of Kildare. St. Brigid's Church was erected recently to serve the newly-built village of Killester. Killester district has belonged for many centuries to the Howth family.

The first turn to the left, having passed the Industrial School, leads, by a road running parallel to the Malahide and Swords Roads, to the latter highway at the village of Cloghran, or, as it is sometimes called, Cloghran Swords, to distinguish it from Cloghran Huddart (locally pronounced 'Heather') in the western part of the county. This road passes another churchyard with another old ruined church dedicated to St. Nicholas. Having passed a *botharin* called Skelly's Lane the townland of Kilmore is traversed. In the garden of a house on the right are two large statues re presenting Queen Victoria and her husband the Prince Consort. These figures, as they represent Victoria and Albert in their youth, may perhaps date from shortly after their marriage on the 10th of February, 1840. Farther on the way to Cloghran a little village called Cock and Rabbit is passed. The name seems to come from the sign of an inn, and, though well-known in Fingal, is never marked on the maps. An eighteenth-century map, how ever, marks Silver Hill and Golden Valley in this district. The well-wooded and secluded district which succeeds is called Clonshagh, anciently Glynshagh.

Following the Malahide Road from Artane we cross, at Artane Bridge, the Naniken River which, rising in Beaumont, falls into the sea after Rowing through the demesne of St. Anne's, Dollymount. The next village is Coolock which gives name to this Barony. It is the largest village on the road, and the church here is dedicated to St. Brendan of Kerry, whose feast occurs on the 16th of May. As already mentioned, Moatfield on the left, with the moat on the lawn, was the residence in boyhood of Charles Lever whose father built the house[81]. On a road parallel to the high road which is reached by the turn on the right beyond Coolock, but more shortly from Raheny, the picturesque ruins of Grange Abbey may be seen. Coolock district belongs to the Domvilles of Santry[82].

The first turn at left some distance beyond Coolock traverses the district of Belcamp, interesting as the birthplace of Henry Grattan. His father's country residence was here and two of his biographers say that he was born here. The others do not commit themselves to any statement on the subject[83].

A subsequent possessor was Sir Edward Newenham, many years member for the County of Dublin. Newenham was a great admirer of George Washington and corresponded with him. Sir Jonah Barrington gives a ludicrous account of this correspondence, but Sir Jonah's statements must often be discounted. There is still at Belcamp, which now belongs to the Oblate Fathers, a small tower with an inscription, built by Newenham in honour of Washington in 1778. That Newenham should have been allowed, by the Government to erect this tower, even on his own grounds, at that time seems somewhat surprising when we consider the condition of things in 1778. Already the War of Independence of the revolted American colonies had been raging for three years[84].

The next village on the Malahide Road is Balgriffin, once the property of the celebrated Red Hugh O'Neill. The next is St. Dolough's, where there is a famous old Church dedicated to that saint, whose feast occurs on the 17th of November. The old Church has a strong stone roof like the Saxon churches, six centuries old and still good. St. Dolough's bed of penance and St. Catherine's Well are also here and an old High Cross. The roof of the Church, which is on a height, commands an extensive and beautiful view. St. Dolough was also the patron of the Church at Cloghran Swords. Passing a country road on the left called Baskin Lane the village of Kinsaley is entered. Here there is a modern Catholic Church, begun in 1832, dedicated to St. Nicholas of Tolentino of the Augustinian Order, whose feast is on the 10th of September. But the old Church here was dedicated for centuries to St. Nicholas of Myra to whom the 6th of December is sacred.

Continuing our course on the high road we pass on the left Abbeville House, often misspelled Abbeyville, built by the powerful John Beresford, who resided here, then the village of Feltrim is reached, and the turn to the left leads to the Hill of Feltrim, the highest eminence of the inland part of Coolock Barony. Feltrim and Effernock belonged to the Fagan family from the middle of the sixteenth century until the forfeitures which followed the Catholic defeat at the Boyne. The house, which has disappeared, was on Feltrim Hill. The summit is now crowned by the ruins of a windmill, a conspicuous object for miles around. The view of Fingal, Portrane, Howth, the sea and the islands is one of the finest in the county. A quarry is on one side of the hill, but the other is still covered with briers, and its wild aspect easily explains the name Feltrim which means 'ridge of wolves'. The pleasant prospect of well-cultivated fields and fine crops is also to be seen in this neighbourhood. In the reign of Elizabeth the Earl of Desmond was committed to the custody of Christopher Fagan of Feltrim who informed the Government that he would not act as his gaoler and generously permitted him to escape to Munster. Not far from Feltrim is the old house of Drynam, built in the reign of Charles I. The Fagans had property in the city near St. Werburgh's Gate, and it is remarkable that in a field to the left of the road which leads from the hill to Swords there is a well of St. Werburgh. St. Werburgh was patroness of a church in Bristol, and Henry II granted Dublin 'to the men of Bristol'. This was the origin of the introduction of her patronage into Dublin. She was a Saxon princess and nun who died in 683 and her feast is kept on the 3rd of February[85].

The highway, passing the fine demesne of Malahide Castle, enters Malahide, a place which is not as well known to Dubliners mid tourists in general as it deserves to be. It is a Station on the Northern Railway within easy reach of Dublin. Lambay Island, Portrane, Donabate, Rush, Lusk, Skerries, Balbriggan and other interesting places in Fingal are not far away. Malahide itself is beautifully situated on the outer corner of a bay formed by the confluence of two rivers. Here are a fine hotel, a good strand, golf links and most interesting coast and inland scenery. Many of the places recently traversed in this sketch, Feltrim, Kinsaley, St. Dolough's, etc., are only a short distance oft. Two miles inland is the interesting old borough of Swords. The road to it passes the ruin of Seatown Castle on the coast, once inhabited by the Russell family.

But the most interesting inland place is the Castle and Demesne of Lord Talbot de Malahide, which is usually open to the public. The title dates from 1831 but the Talbot family have been in possession of Malahide since 1174. The oldest part of the Castle is as old as that time. It contains an antique room wainscotted with Irish oak, but its chief ornament is the picture gallery which includes several old historical pictures, the most famous being a picture of the Nativity of Our Lord, which was once an altar-piece in the Chapel of Holyrood Palace and belonged to Mary Queen of Scots. It is said to have been painted by Albert Durer. In the ruined chapel beside the Castle is the tomb of the wife of Sir Richard Talbot who lived in the fifteenth century. This was Maud Plunkett who had been previously married to Hussey, son of the Baron of Galtrim in Meath, who was slain on his wedding day. On this incident is founded Gerald Griffin's ballad, *The Bridal of Malahide*[86]. Malahide Demesne has as magnificent specimens of forest trees as are to be found in the British Isles. Near Malahide is Sea Park, built by Nicholas Morres who married a lady of the Talbot family. His son was in the Irish Brigade. The new water supply of the town is from the Ward River. There is a little harbour with some trade in coal and salt, and an oyster-bed.

As there are Lombard and French names beside Swords so the Spanish and Quixotic name of La Mancha is found beside Malahide, and the warlike Spanish name of Talavera just outside Baldoyle. The latter is evidently called after the town of Talavera della Reyna on the Tagus where Sir Arthur Wellesley, afterwards Duke of Wellington, defeated the French in July, 1809, exactly one hundred and twenty-three years ago.

The most attractive environs of Malahide are those on the sea, which is here overhung, as well as the town, by the eminence called Carrick Hill.

But take the coast road from the town, and in a short time the old tower of Robertswall Castle is reached. This warden of a lonely shore was erected by the De Birminghams in the fifteenth century. It stands on a bold rocky coast where there was a well-called Tubbermaclaney which has disappeared, though there is now another spring not far away. As if by enchantment the rough precipitous shore suddenly gives place to the beautiful Velvet Strand, one of the greatest beauty spots of the County Dublin and still too little known, although it has been much frequented by motorists for the last few years. Portmarnock Railway Station is quite convenient to it. To see it all it should be entered by the way called Ferny Gutter. There are two other entrances called Church Gap and Caulfield's Gap. Not only is this Strand the finest to be found for many miles from Dublin, but its outlook is unique. Lambay is not very distant and Ireland's Eye shoots its rocky mass precipitous up from the ocean at apparently a stone's throw. The aspect of Howth too from this point will be found quite unfamiliar by those who usually view the headland from the southern or city side.

John D'Alton does not mention the name, although it existed when he wrote, of the Velvet Strand, but his pleasure in it was extreme, and he seems, like many a Dublin resident of today, to have come upon it by surprise, and to have written of it as a discovery. His description is worth quoting: 'Presently valleys of dazzling sands appeared opening to the sea, and in some places exhibiting a scanty vegetation, but more usually the bare tracks of rabbits. Then such a lovely strand, so white, so firm, so curiously inlaid with every specimen of shells; the silent sunny sandy cliffs at left; the blue sea at right, foaming its white wreaths over the whole shore, and in the distance Howth, apparently insulated, and Ireland's Eye, and further yet Lambay enveloped in vapour. The black rocky shore of Tobbermackeany succeeded, its dangerous aspect being fatally illustrated by the masts of a sunken vessel, that pointed above the full tide at a short distance from its ledge, arid over which the gulls were wildly screaming'.

Portmarnock derives its name from the same saint as Robert Burn's Kilmarnock in Ayrshire. The Plunketts have lived in Portmarnock for many years. Students of Fingallian antiquities will observe how many old castles belonged to the Plunketts and the Barnewalls. The latter are Normans of the Pale, but the Plunketts are Scandinavian, probably Norwegians like most Fingallians and not descended from the Danes. The Plunketts are known to have been in Ireland at least a century before the Norman invasion, and one family of them bears the title Earl of Fingall. Other Scandinavian surnames in Fingal are Segrave, Seaver, Sweetman (Swedeman), Harold, Dowdall, Derham, Harford, Dromgoole and Hamlet. The surnames of Fottrell, Yourell, Butterly and Bobbett, found mostly in Fingal, are also probably of like origin. Most of the inhabitants of North County Dublin, like those of the northern half of Leinster in general, bear surnames indicative of Ulster origin. The Scandinavian Kingdom of Dublin was founded in 852 and lasted over three centuries. While it lasted St. Mary's Abbey, Christ Church, St. Michan's and many other churches were founded and Dublin began to be an important city.

The ruin of the old Church at Portmarnock exhibits a belfry pierced to swing two bells. This singular arrangement of a double belfry is almost peculiar to Fingal, being found in many churches of the district[87]. Approaching Baldoyle from Portmarnock there is a ferry to the Portmarnock Golf Links across the inlet. This arm of the sea separates the mainland from the long sandy peninsula of Portmarnock which terminates in Portmarnock Point opposite Cush Point in Sutton. Baldoyle is widely known for its racecourse, and is the property of the Corporation of Dublin to whom it was granted in reward for its opposition to the rebellion of Silken Thomas. Returning from Baldoyle the village of Raheny is passed. It is pleasantly situated on the Santry River, and the church erected by Lord Ardilaun is worthy of attention for its architecture.

CHAPTER XVI

CLONTARF

T HE LAST HIGHWAY FROM THE north side of the city is that which leads by the seashore to Clontarf and Howth, a district with the cheerful distinction of the lowest death-rate in Dublin. The road to Clontarf and Howth is very well known to Dubliners owing to the excellent tram service. The name of Clontarf at once recalls the great battle on which Gray has founded his ode of the *Fatal Sisters*. It was fought on Good Friday, the 23rd of April, 1014, and the Scandinavian power was finally broken by the great Irish King, Brian Boroimhe, who was killed by the Danish admiral, Broder, an apostate, it is said, from Christianity. The best authorities assert that this battle was fought about the mouth of the Tolka and near the northern outskirts of the city; but there was hard fighting about Marino, and the battle went on as far east as the site of Castle Avenue. Some vestiges of Tomar's Wood remain, mentioned in accounts of the battle, especially at Marino and near Clontarf Castle, where Brian's two-handed sword is still preserved.

Many names of places in Clontarf recall the battle, such as Brian Boroimhe's Well, in Castle Avenue; Boroimhe Lodge, facing the Bull Wall; Brian Boru Avenue; Turlough Terrace near Annesley Bridge, called after Brian's grandson, who met his death here; Danesfield, Dollymount, where a Danish sword was dug up in 1830; Danesfort near Castle Avenue; Cencora, Castle Avenue; Conquer Hill, the slope beside Crab Lake, which is a pond in the field behind Boroimhe Lodge; Conquer Hill Cottage, Dollymount; Conquer Hill Road and Conquer Terrace; Kinkora, also at Dollymount, and Danespark. Sitric was the Danish commander in the battle. It is said that there were many killed at the Danish 'fishing weir of Clontarf', where Ballybough Bridge is now, and that many were drowned there. It has been calculated that the tide must have served at five minutes to ix o'clock on the day of the battle

Clontarf is supposed to have derived its name, 'plain of the bull', like the North and South Bulls, from the roaring of the sea[88]. There used to be an oyster-bed on the bank called the Furlong. Clontarf has been in the City of Dublin since the Boundaries Act passed in 1900. It seems strange that a sequestered spot in the Green Lanes should have been in the city while Rathmines Road and Pembroke Road were not. The Corporation have, however, done much for Clontarf, and will, no doubt, make this handsome suburb worthy of the city ownership. They have reclaimed the fore- shore from the Tolka mouth at Annesley Bridge to the Railway Bridge at Clontarf and are making a promenade of reclaimed land beyond that point. However attractive the result may he the process is necessarily unpleasant.

Many names in Clontarf, which date from the early years of the nineteenth century, are worthy of attention. Tokay is called after the town in Hungary where the wine comes from. Rosetta recalls Egypt and Simla India. Warrenpoint, with its sphinx-guarded gate, is called from owners of property, and is near a point in the coast (once called Cockle Point) like Seapoint lower down. There was formerly a house in Clontarf called Cockle Hall. Winston Ville behind the Crescent. and Blandford Lodge on the shore seem to intimate some connection with the Marlborough family.

Sir Winston Churchill, who lived some time in Dublin, was father of the great Duke, and the name Winston has been used by the Churchills since one of them married a Gloucestershire Winston. Blandford is the second title of the Duke of Marlborough, but the name of the house may come from Blandford in Dorsetshire from which the title is derived.

The house called Grace Dieu seems to be named after the place north of Swords where the Canonesses of St. Augustine had their great Convent of Our Lady of the Nativity. This was the largest convent of nuns in the County of Dublin, famous for its great extent and large community. Vernon Avenue, Vernon Parade and Mount Vernon are called after the family so long proprietors of the district, but the last name reproduces that of Washington's house in Virginia. Haddon Road, as has been said, is from the association of the Vernon family with Haddon in Derbyshire. But it is very unlikely that

Dollymount takes its name from that Dorothy Vernon, the daughter of Sir George of Haddon, the King of the Peak, who married Sir John Manners. The name Dollymount, first applied to a house, was afterwards bestowed on a village or seaside resort which sprang up beside it.

Some other names of more recent origin are also interesting. In so Conservative a district we are not surprised to meet with Hughenden, called from Hughenden in Buckinghamshire, so long the residence of the Earl of Beaconsfield, who was also Viscount Hughenden. Mentana recalls the place in Italy where the troops of Napoleon III defeated the Garibaldian invaders of the Papal States on the 3rd of November, 1867. A house in Marino Avenue (marked 'Charter Row' on old maps) near the Howth Road end has been called Bleak House for some years past, thus adding another to the Dickens memorials about Dublin. It may be objected that Bleak House in the story is far inland at St. Albans in Hertfordshire. But it is known that the real Bleak House is on the coast, at Broadstairs, a favourite summer resort of the novelist. The name of Snugborough, off Vernon Avenue, is not taken from Dickens, but it is such a name as might occur in his works. He goes as near it as Dullborough.

The Howth Road leaves the shore at the Crescent and rejoins it beyond Raheny. At a little distance from the shore the Great Northern Railway Company opened a station about twenty-five years ago for Clontarf, a welcome recognition of the growing suburb. This spot was formerly called the Black Quarry. The Presbyterian Church on the sea road was built about forty years ago. Beyond the Railway, Kingscourt House is passed. This old building was the Royal Charter School, erected in 1749. It was afterwards used as baths. Hollybrook Park and the newly-made Hollybrook Road represent an old name here, derived, from the little stream which flows into the sea at Brookside, near Strandville. Avenue. St. Lawrence Road is from the surname of the Howth, family, proprietors of Killester. The road forms part of the narrow strip of that parish and townland which stretches to the sea.

Castle Avenue, which was the central road of Clontarf Township, runs from the sea to the gate of Clontarf Castle, and beyond that, having the Castle demesne at left and those of Yew Park arid Blackheath at right, to the Howth Road, which it meets at Furry Park, near Killester. In the demesne, to the north-west of the Castle, is St. Philip's Well, called St. Dennis's Well on the older Ordnance Map of 1837. The reason for the change is not evident. The first castle built here was erected a few years after the Norman Invasion by Adam de Phepoe, a favourite of the famous Hugh de Lacy. The old Castle, becoming ruinous, was demolished in 1835 and the present erected on its site. The gate is adorned with the boar, the heraldic cognizance of the Vernons, and with the family motto, *Vernon semper viret*. Vernon always flourishes. Some works on heraldry give another reading to the motto, in a kind of punning variant: *Ver non semper viret*. Spring does not always flourish.

From Castle Avenue there are two entrances to the Green Lanes of Clontarf, so famous for pretty sylvan scenery. One is by Seafield Avenue, and the other by Verville, formerly Fairville, to Vernon Avenue. The first meets the sea a little beyond the entrance to the Bull Wall. At the end of its course is the fine old house of Seafield which gives name to the avenue. But at the beginning and quite' close to the Castle, is Clontarf Protestant Church, whose spire is one of the most conspicuous objects in the view of Dublin Bay. Where the Church and Castle stand there once stood a Cornmandery of the Knights Templars, which was granted, upon the suppression of that Order, to the Order of Knights Hospitallers, called Knights of St. John of Jerusalem. This Order derived its name from St. John the Baptist, to whose honour its founders had built a Chapel at Jerusalem. The old patron of Clontarf in ancient Irish days was St. Comgall, whose feast day is the 10th of May. But since the Knights of St. John settled here, so many centuries ago, the parish has been dedicated to St. John the Baptist. The former Town Hall has been happily transformed into the Church of St. Anthony, to supply the needs of the rapidly- growing population of the western portion of the parish.

Passing on by the coast road a strange object meets the eye, a little distance out on the strand. This is a cylindrical wall which once enclosed the shaft of a lead mine. The mine was discovered in 1756 and worked for some time, but had to be abandoned owing to the invasions of the tide. Just beyond this but farther out to sea are the Clontarf Baths and Assembly Rooms. This is a favourite resort of Dublin bathers, being so near the city and convenient in every way. There is a swimming club which holds an annual gala. The Secretary of the Baths Company is also Secretary of the Lifeboat Institution for Clontarf District. Near this is the ground of the Clontarf Tennis Club. The Cricket and Football Clubs have their ground in Castle Avenue. Yachting and golf have their allotted quarters farther on.

A square planted with trees in front of Strand House, a Convent and School of the Holy Faith, and the Catholic Parish Church of St. John the Baptist are passed before Vernon Avenue is reached. The church is over ninety years old. Vernon Avenue is the centre of the old fishing village of Clontarf and of the Green Lanes. A very large part of Clontarf, coast and inland, is in the townland of Greenlanes. Convent House in Vernon Avenue was, for some years before 1819, the Convent of the Dominican Nuns who came here from Channel Row (North Brunswick Street) and left this for Cabra. Castilla recalls a Spanish alliance of the Bradstreet family who have lived there so long.

The coast road at the foot of Vernon Avenue still called Clontarf Sheds from sheds which once stood here for curing fish. Captain Perry's Map of Dublin Bay and Harbour in 1728, marks 'Herring Sheds' at this point. A little farther on, at Fortview and Fortview Avenue, names taken from the obsolete Pigeon House Fort on the South Wall opposite, the old houses are gracefully ornamented with ironwork. Fingal Avenue near this and Fingal Terrace, Howth Road, may be regarded as still another historic memorial. In ancient Ireland the old name of this district, showing the Scandinavian origin of its inhabitants, is closely associated with the Battle of Clontarf, which took place within its bounds. There is an old Irish march, still well known, called *The Return from Fingal*, in commemoration of the victorious march of Brian's Dalcassian army back to Clare. It is quite different from the better known *Brian Boroimhe's March*. Beside Fingal Avenue is still another Belvedere, long the headquarters of the Clontarf Yacht and Boat Club. The annual Regatta, a most popular fixture with Dubliners, takes place in that part of the bay which faces this eastern end of Clontarf, necessarily bounded by the Bull Wall. In a field near the Tramway Company's Station is the pond called Crab Lake and the slight eminence sloping down to it called Conquer Hill.

The view southward from any height in Fingal or the north side of the city terminates in the Dublin Mountains. But the range is seen to peculiar advantage from Clontarf strand or the Bull Wall. In one direction the city appears with all its spires, towers and chimneys, Dublin Harbour and its shipping being nearest. The long South Wall and Poolbeg Lighthouse seem quite close by. All Dublin Bay, with Dun Laoghaire Harbour, occupies the foreground, and the Irish Sea stretches beyond. At one side are Howth and Ireland's Eye. Looking to the opposite side the whole panorama of the Dublin Mountains displays itself. The nearer and higher hills may be distinguished on a clear day. Slievenabawnogue, Montpelier, with the ruins of Speaker Conolly's shooting-lodge on top, Killakee, Cruagh, Tibradden, Kilmashogue and the Two and Three Rock Mountains are the most easily identified. To the left of these appear the Golden Spears, Carrickgollogan, marked by the chimney of Ballycorus Lead Mine on its summit, and farthest to the left Killiney with its three hills and two obelisks, one on the highest point erected in the hard year 1741; the smaller and lower at Ballybrack marking the spot where John Sackville, the fourth Duke of Dorset, was killed hunting on the 14th of June, 1815, at the early age of twenty-one.

The Bull Wall, which, with the South Wall, confines Dublin Harbour, was erected more than one hundred years ago. This long pier was meant to quicken the speed of the ebbing tide and make the Liffey current run with greater force in narrower limits. It has undoubtedly done much towards lessening the disadvantage of Dublin Bar to the Port; by freeing the channel from obstacles and creating a smooth and straight approach to the Harbour. The extreme portion of this breakwater is very rudely constructed. From shore to point it is now not far from two miles long a lighthouse terminates it and the beacons and buoys of Dublin Port are all within sight of it. It has long been a favourite bathing place with Dubliners, but has lately become more of a promenade, for which it is well adapted. Its bridge spans the narrow ribbon of sea which flows by Dollymount and the North Bull, and is called Crablake Water, formerly Raheny Lake.

Ordnance Survey Maps give the name of Cold Harbour to the angle between the Coast Guard Station and the shore at Seafield Avenue, but maps of a century ago apply this name to the inland pond of Crab Lake in the field between Seafield Avenue and the shore road. The North Bull is an island of great extent, being about two miles long and more than three hundred and eighty-five acres in extent. The part near the bridge belongs to the Most Rev, the Hon. B. J. Plunket, and the farther part to the Howth family. The greater portion of it is only about a century old. The former Coast Guard Station and Golf Club House serve to dispel the idea of solitude it naturally calls up. It is introduced effectively by Lever into *The O'Donoghue*. This sandy island is covered with a poor marine vegetation and frequented by sea-birds. On the eastern, or side next the open sea, is a beautiful smooth strand strewn with shells, particularly with the long smooth double one of the razor-fish. It is a great advantage to Dubliners to have such a beach within easy distance by tram of the centre of the city. The North Bull and its pier are sure to share in the growing popularity of Clontarf.

MORNING

LEO ealPINE*

Cardura.

Allopurinol

Eltroxin

Comfort Eye Drops

Night.

Atorvastatin

Eye drop Gainsher

Continuing the tram road from the Bull Wall entrance, Dollymount is reached. This was a separate village some years ago, but a great number of new houses have been built, and it is now almost connected with Clontarf. The name appears as that of a separate country seat in a book of reference a little more than ninety years old. Crablake Water, the ribbon of permanent sea before alluded to, flows in front of Dollymount, where many pleasure boats are kept. This ribbon connects the part of Dublin Harbour which is always covered, even at the lowest tides, with the open sea at Howth, and is largely maintained by three streams which discharge their waters into it, the little Naniken River, flowing out through St. Anne's, the Santry River coming down from Raheny, and Dollymount proper may be said to lie between Seafield Avenue and Blackbush Lane. Visitors will find a convenient Hotel here. At one end of Dollymount is Baymount Castle, a handsome castellated suburban house. The wall and gate lodge are also battlemented. There was a fine row of old elms by the wall in the Green Lane behind it. The Castle is now a School, but ninety years ago it was the residence of Dr. Traill, Protestant Bishop of Down and Connor. More than half a century ago it was the seat of one of the earliest Loreto Convents, but Mrs. Ball, the foundress of the Order, abandoned the foundation owing to a destructive fire which broke out here.

Some place-names in Dollymount arc worthy of attention. The little old avenue called Telledan has a name appearing on various maps at various dates as Telladan, Telleden and Tellendon. Its origin appears to be unfathomable. Lakeview is so called from the view of Crablake Water, but the first syllable would have spoiled the name. Hassendean is the more. correct form of the word familiar to many in Scott's song, *Jock O' Hazeldean*. A name disappeared here about twenty years ago which might have been spared. It was evidently conferred by an admirer of Tennyson. This was Enid Cottage, called after Enid the Good, one of the best of the heroines of the Arthurian legends.

Just beyond Dollymount is St. Anne's, the residence of the Most Rev, the Hon. B. J. Plunket. There is no finer demesne within an equal distance of the metropolis, whether as regards extent or beauty. It has been in possession of the Guinness family for upwards of ninety years. The name of a townland here is Blackbush or Heronstown, and the demesne bore both of those names formerly as well as that of Thornhill. Old maps mark it Heronstown and D'Alton refers to it as 'Blackbush, the seat of Mr. Guinness'. Sir Benjamin

Guinness bestowed its present worthier name on this estate, in 1837 probably from the ancient holy well of St. Anne which is included within its limits.

Blackbush Lane, which skirts the southern boundary wall of St. Anne's, has recently been named Mount Prospect Avenue, from the house of Mount Prospect, occupied as an auxiliary by the North William Street Orphanage of the Sisters of Charity. From this road the Green Lanes may be entered at their eastern extremity, or Raheny may be reached by Wade's Lane.

Continuing on the road to Howth beyond St. Anne's, Watermill Road is passed. At the end of this road, which leads to Raheny, is Watermill Bridge over the mouth of the Santry River. A little before this Naniken Bridge is crossed where the little Naniken River discharges, its waters. A little farther on, at a point where an inland road meets the tram-road, a third little stream flows in. This spot is called The Whip of the Water. There was a stone built into a house at Watermill Bridge, bearing the letters C.E. (Civitas Eblana) to show that this was the boundary of the City of Dublin. That point was not conceded by the owners of property here; and, even under the Boundaries Act, the limits of Dublin still fall a little short of this locality.

The road passes a low flat district, of which the land is salt-marsh, and the only interesting object is the ruined church of Kilbarrack, once called the Chapel of Mone, belonging to St. Mary's Abbey and afterwards to Howth. It was the chapel formerly of the people who went 'down to the in ships'. The churchyard adjoining is chiefly notable as the burying-place of Francis Higgins, called from an early incident in his career the Sham Squire. He was a somewhat unscrupulous adventurer who managed to obtain a questionable political prominence in Dublin in the last troubled years of the eighteenth century. But his career and his burying-place were becoming alike forgotten when both leaped into sudden prominence in the year 1866 by the publication of the very interesting *Sham Squire* of the late Dr. William John Fitzpatrick. One amusing testimony to the great success and popularity of the book was the transfer of the historic nickname from Higgins to the amiable author.

CHAPTER XVII

HOWTH

WE HAVE NOW REACHED THE district of Sutton, the threshold of Howth. Sutton Railway Station is situated at the narrowest point of the isthmus connecting Howth with the mainland, for it must be remembered that Howth is land apart, at once a peninsula and a promontory. The development of Sutton, which comprises the isthmus and the western side of the Hill of Howth, has been quite phenomenal in the last forty years. Nor can this be wondered at when we consider its great beauty and its mild climate. The latter is due to its sheltered position, the Hill acting as a barrier to the cold easterly breezes. This side of the Hill recalls the Mediterranean coast of Italy. A road leading to the steep where the village of Sancer once was, passes the little ruined Church and Well of St. Fintan, who is commemorated on the 17th of February.

The railway and the tram both lead to the town of Howth, where fishing is still the principal occupation of the permanent inhabitants. Both train and tram pass Corr Castle, the remnant of the old residence of the Lords Howth. The harbour, built a hundred and fifteen years ago, at a cost of half a million, soon became a failure as its position was ill-chosen. It is said that it would have been a great success if constructed a little to the east ward in the Bay of Balscadden, which is the Fingallian form Bal (for Bally), a town, and the Irish word for herrings. The Baths of Howth are situated in Balscadden Bay. It is called Bolskatin in Lever's *Tom Burke*. The building of Howth Harbour figures humorously in Samuel Lover's amusing Irish tale,

Barney O'Reardon the Navigator. The Lighthouse and Lifeboat and Coast Guard Stations are on the Pier.

At a distance of about a mile and a quarter from the harbour is the rocky and picturesque little island of Ireland's Eye, the property o the Howth family, but formerly belonging to the Archbishops of Dublin. Its form resembles a cone, and it is a kind of natural breakwater to Howth Harbour. The landing-place is at Carrigeen Bay on the western side. The island contains 53 acres 24 perches (Ordnance Survey, 1837), or 58 acres 3 roods 5 perches (Ordnance Survey, 1877) of wild rocky mountain sheep pasture and tall fern and undergrowth. It is uninhabited, and its only buildings are a Martello Tower[89] and the little ruined church said to have been founded in the sixth century. The old name of the island was Inismacnessain, the island of the sons of Nessan, and three of these holy men, who lived here, were commemorated on the 15th of March. Some of the cliffs of Ireland's Eye are exceedingly bold and striking in form, suggesting strong fortifications. Carrigeen, Thulla, the Steer and the Rowan Rocks are the names of some of the more remarkable cliffs, islets, and headlands, while one deep inlet, beside the last-named rocks, once called the Long Hole, has acquired a new name from a tragedy of which it was the scene about eighty years ago.

The Hill of Howth, as it is popularly called, is one of the limits of Dublin Bay, the other boundary being Sorrento Point at Dalkey, nearly seven miles distant. The old Irish name was Ben Edair, the hill of Edar, a personal name. The Hill is a conspicuous object for many miles on land and sea[90]. It is the most prominent feature of the North County Dublin. It is a simile in Thomas Hood's *Ode to Rae Wilson*: 'Tis not as plain as the old Hill of Howth' It is a sort of barometer, as may be perceived from the county proverb: 'If Howth has a black cap, Fingal may look out'. The summit of Howth, now easily attainable by the tramway constructed by the Great Northern Railway Company, commands a most extensive view, comprising not only the usual Dublin Bay prospect of sea, city and mountains, but also the distant peaked Mourne Mountains in Down more than sixty miles away. Slieve Donard, the highest, may be made out, and the round-topped Slieve Gullion in Armagh, more like the Wicklow Mountains in form. The latter is easily identified because it is some distance away from the Mourne Range. In very favourable circumstances even the sharp summits of the Cambrian Range may be seen on the horizon. It may appear surprising that Wales should be seen from Ireland, but the County Dublin coast heights, such as Lambay, Howth, the Three Rock, Killiney and Bray Head, all afford this view in very clear weather at early morning or at sunset. The top of Snowdon, over three thousand feet high, with the Pass of Llanberis beside it in Carnarvon, and Cader Idris, the high mountain in Merioneth, are the most easily discernible of the Welsh Mountains.

The name of Howth is from the Scandinavian Hoved, a head. The Danes have left memorials of their stay in many place-names on the east coast of Ireland, such as Strangford, Carlingford Lambay (Lamb Island), Ireland's Eye, Howth, Dalkey, Wicklow, Wexford and Waterford. Some of the Howth place-names surpass in singularity those of any other place in this county. Sancer before-mentioned is now called the townland of Censure, an odd Anglicization of an Irish word. Bottle Quay is also on the Sutton side. On the Hill are Cowbooter Lane, Boggeen Lane, Mudoak Rock and, in Howth Castle Demesne, Black Jack's Well and the Bloody Stream. At the north east angle there is Puck's Rock, where St. Nessan struck the devil, according to a local legend; the Nose of Howth coming next, the north-east part of the coast. The Nose is not far from Irelands Eye; but the corresponding north-east point of Lambay is also called the Nose. Along the wild bold East Cliff, the following odd names of rocks, bays and headlands succeed each other from north to south; Green Ivy, The Piper's Gut (Pifa Gut is a channel in the Farne Islands, England), Highroom Bed, Lough Leven, Gaskin's Leap and Webb's Castle Rock. The resemblance of cliffs and rocks to castles has often been noticed[91].

In the town of Howth which is still, despite some modern improvements, a fishing village, the picturesque ruins of the old Collegiate Church, usually but incorrectly styled Howth Abbey, are conspicuous. It may well be said that this building shines by contrast with its surroundings. It was dedicated to the Blessed Virgin. Its architecture is of the Gothic order, which is not common in the County of Dublin. The original foundation is said to have been on Ireland's Eye, and the transfer was made soon after the Howth family settled here.

Howth Castle, which is seen when approaching from Dublin, and also from the top of the Hill, is a Norman keep of the Middle Ages, modified by some additions in accordance with modern taste. The Castle and Demesne are open to the public on stated days in the summer, when the long old hail, with the armoury and Sir Almeric Tristram's two-handed sword may be inspected. The rhododendrons in the garden here are quite famous. The founder of the family was the brave Norman knight just mentioned, the companion in arms of the celebrated De Courcy. He settled here in 1177 and defeated some Danes, who then owned Howth, in battle near a mountain stream on the Hill. The lands thus acquired by the sword were confirmed to the family by King John. It is said that Sir Almeric Tristram fought this battle on the 10th of August, the feast of St. Laurence the Martyr, and that he assumed the surname of St. Lawrence, borne by his descendants to this day, in memory of the circumstance. But this tradition is rendered doubtful by the record of the surname of St. Laurent in France before the Norman Conquest of England, and by its recurrence in Hampshire some years after that event. There is a monument in a Church at Rouen to a Saint Laurens who died in 1560 and, as we are told that Sir Almeric and Courcy had made in a Church in Rouen a romantic compact of chivalry, under taking to achieve fortune by their swords, it would seem that after all the surname is probably of Norman origin. On the death of the late Earl of Howth the St. Lawrence property fell to his nephew, Mr. Julian C. Gaisford-St. Lawrence of Offington, Sussex. The late peer was fourth Earl and thirtieth Baron. The Earldom dated from 1767, the Barony from 1177, being, perhaps, the oldest title existing. Some books of reference on titled families marked 'No heir to earldom', implying that there was one to the barony. One would expect that so ancient a title could not easily die out. The crest in the coat-of-arms is a sea lion, the supporters a sea lion and a mermaid, in allusion probably to the situation of the family possessions. The shield bears two swords in saltire with four roses. The mysterious motto is *Qui Panse*.

Of so old a family there are, as might be expected, many legends. The best known is regarded as quite authentic. In 1575 the celebrated Grace O'Malley, Chieftainess of Burrishoole in Mayo, landed here and found the gates closed during dinner. Indignant at what she considered a want of hospitality, she seized the boy heir of Lord Howth and conveyed him on her galley to her home in Mayo. She returned him only on condition of a promise from Lord Howth that the gates should be left open during dinner in future. This concondition was observed until a little over a hundred years ago. There is a picture in the Castle representing the carrying off of the heir.

Another legend asserts that one of the Lords of Howth was married to a lady of unknown and mysterious origin who was cast ashore by the tide.

There is an old tree in the demesne called the St. Lawrence Tree, to which a legend is also attached.

Although Kingstown Harbour superseded Howth as a packet station and place of landing after George IV had landed here on the 12th of August, 1821, his fifty-ninth birthday, Howth has revived its prosperity in another way in our own day. It has lately been constituted an Urban District. It shares with Clontarf, as has been said, the pleasant distinction of possessing the lowest death-rate in the neighbourhood of Dublin. Many terraces have been built not far from the town, while the finest new houses are springing up on all parts of the Hill. A stranger revisiting Howth after forty years would scarcely recognize it for the lonely and primitive place he had previously known. Although much remains to be done, especially in the town, as the old fishing village is called, still there has been wonderful progress. The number of new houses and new roads alone is a good test of this and hotel accommodation is also greatly improved. There are golf links at Sutton, Portmarnock, and even on Howth Hill itself.

The summit of the Hill is Black Linn, which is 563 feet above the sea. The Hill proper is, of course, the eastern part of the peninsula. This is best seen by traversing the New Path, overhanging the East Cliff and starting from a quarry, not in appropriately named Kilrock. It may be remarked that, beside the ores of lead, copper and iron, that rare mineral, manganese, is also found here. The New Path conducts to the Bailey Lighthouse on the ever verdant peninsula of the Green Bailey. This was called formerly Dun Criomthain from the name of an Irish king residing here who fought the Romans in Britain. The present lighthouse was built in 1814. The other principal heights of the Hill are the peaked top of Shelmartin, the best point for a good view, and the lower heights of Carrickmore and Carrickbrack, the latter over hanging The Needles. On the west of the Hill is a Cromlech.

There is no place near Dublin more assured of a prosperous future than Howth. Nor is this wonderful. It is the gem of Fingal; and may even be described as the most beautiful place near Dublin. Here is the great attraction to a citizen of escape from roads, and the still greater of hills, vales and streams, furze, fern, and heather. Writing ninety years ago the historian of the County said of Howth 'were it within six times the distance from London that it is from Dublin, it would long before this be a diadem of picturesque attraction'. All Irishmen of the present day will acknowledge that it has at last become so.

ENDNOTES

1 The aspect of the north side of Dublin was greatly changed in the eighteenth century by the construction of the Circular Road in 1768, and of the Royal Canal in 1791.

2 The four Courts absorbed Arch Lane, which seems to have been called Purfictor Alley afterwards. Morgan place is of the same age as the four Courts. King James II's Irish Parliament was held in the old Four Courts in 1689.

3 A very interesting History of the King's Hospital was published by the late Sir Frederick Falkiner, many years Recorder of Dublin.

4 Another account says on St. Stephen's Green.

5 The earlier Scandinavian Kings of Dublin were addicted to piracy and, like their fellow-countryman, Godred Crovan, King of Man, who captured Dublin on one occasion, used to go on Viking expeditions. Those who are interested in this period of the history of our city cannot do better than consult Haliday's *History of the Scandinavian Kingdom of Dublin*.

6 The Carmelite nuns now in Ranelagh had theft convent in Pudding Lane, now Lincoln Lane, a few doors from No. 12, in the eighteenth century. It was behind No. 16 or 17 Arran Quay.

7 Near Dublin the Ellises also owned Pickardstown and the Boot Inn, about six miles from the General Post Office, on the road to Naul. The title Viscount Clifden passed in 1899 to Lord Robartes in Cornwall, who is connected with Ireland only by descent, but the property fell to lady Annaly, a member of the Agar-Ellis Family.

8 The sign of the well-known Royal Oak tavern here is scarcely true to historic facts. One error is the omission from the picture of colonel careless, who, in honour of his association with Charles II, afterwards changed his name to Carlos, the Spanish for Charles. Careless was with the King in the oak at Boscobel all that 6th of September, 1651, three days after Worcester Field. Nor was the King ever in such immediate jeopardy as is depicted here. But we must remember that John D'Alton in 1838 saw a Royal Oak sign in Swords representing 'King Charles blazing in scarlet and gold through its ill-furnished branches, and a whole regiment bivouacking at its foot'.

9 In the same way Bumbailiff's Lane, off New Street, on the south side; became the meaningless Fumbally's Lane. There was another Hangman's Lane from Kimmage to Dolphin's Barn, where Tom Galvin, the hangman of '98, is said to have lived. It is now called the Dark Lane. Dublin also contained .such names as Cut throat Lane, Murdering Lane, cutpurse Row (corn Market), Hell, near Christ Church, Hog Hill (St. Andrew Street), The Common Lane (Watery Lane, now Brookfield Avenue), Gallows Road, Gallows Hill, Gibbet Meadow, Dirty Lane (Bridgefoot Street and Temple Lane South), Dunghill Lane (Island Street) and Pinchgut Lane. Some eighteenth century street-names were even coarser; yet, they were the recognized official names, figuring in postal addresses, and found in maps and directories. The age of refinement was yet to come, and it has already reached its extreme point in renaming Dublin streets and lanes.

10 By the late Right Hon. John Edward Walsh, Master of the Rolls. It is a most interesting little book, describing the wild Ireland of 1787 and some time later, as depicted by Charles Lever. *The Maybush* and the *Baiting of Lord Althans's* Bull both contained in *Ireland a Hundred and Twenty Years Ago* (Gill, Dublin), are choice specimens of slang, and good illustrations of the coarseness of the age already mentioned.

11 The junctions of King Street with Bolton Street, Church Street with Coleraine Street, Taaffe's village with North Strand, are other instances.

12 Most people know that Wolseley was a native of Dublin, but few are aware that John Churchill, afterwards Duke of Marlborough, resided for several years of his boyhood in our city. His father; Sir Winston Churchill, a Devonshire Cavalier, who had suffered great losses for Charles I in the Civil War, was recompensed by Charles II, shortly after his Restoration,

by a Government appointment in Dublin Castle. Sir Winston's famous son, John, went to school at the Dublin Schoolhouse in Schoolhouse Lane. His favourite classical work is said to have been Vegetius's *Epifome Rei Militaris*, which is not allowed by the Intermediate Education Board to the rising generation of strategists. The Churchill family resided in Lower Bridge Street, then very fashionable, and at that time the approach to the only bridge leading to the north side of Dublin. Thus a great British general, who was an Englishman, had nevertheless some association with Dublin, in which Wellington and Wolseley were born.

13 The name is probably imitated from that of Constitution Hill in London. The names of Smithfield, Pudding Lane, Curzon Street, Fleet Street, Temple Bar, Pimlico, Watling Street, London Bridge, Corn Hill, Drury Lane (now Street), Pye Corner, Spitalfields, Beggar's Bush and Goose Green seem to have a like origin.

14 It cannot be forgotten besides, that, in the first half of the eighteenth century, Lord Chesterfield stands almost alone as the only prominent Englishman who showed some sympathy or kindness to the oppressed catholic majority of the Irish people. There arc some whimsical manifestations of this kindness to be found in the amusing account of his viceroyalty in Mitchel's, *History of Ireland*. Although it is true, as Mitchel says, that he was sent here to conciliate the Catholics lest they might join in the Highland Jacobite insurrection of Prince Charles Edward in 1745, yet it is obvious from his expressions that the policy of allowing the Catholics to exercise their religion openly, in spite of the Penal Laws, was in accordance with his personal opinion, chesterfield said Ireland was ground down by 'deputies of deputies of deputies'. Not withstanding the well-known faults of his character his Irish vice- royalty remains one of the best parts of his life, and a kind of oasis in the desert of persecution. The only other prominent Englishman of that age who sympathized with the Irish Catholics was, strangely enough, Dr. Samuel Johnson, a man of very different character, with whom Chesterfield was at memorable variance.

15 Sir William Wilde supposed this Cromlech to be a monument of the Firbolgs, who inhabited Ireland two thousand years ago. A smaller Cromlech, discovered in a sandpit at Chapelizod, has he set up in the Zoological Gardens.

16 Dr. Joyce also (Irish Names of Places, p. 39) places the Fionn Uisge spring near the Phoenix Column.

17 D'Alton's style, in one of its most extreme flights, is to be seen in his description of Ballyfermot, south of Chapelizod, where he is denouncing a practice not yet extinct in 1838 when he wrote : 'the graveyard exhibits traces of exhumation most revolting to the feelings, and which must powerfully recommend to the selection of surviving relatives, the solemn repose and Security of those sepulchral vaults, where sacrilegious insults cannot be perpetrated, those subterranean chambers that extend themselves within the echoes of holy harmony, and are sealed down from garish intrusion by the superincumbent temple of the Deity'.

18 He was Viscount Tully and Baron Rosberry, both in Kildare.

19 Henry Luttrell, who betrayed the Irish Jacobite cause in 1691, was murdered in 1717 - shot in his sedan chair outside his house in Stafford Street. He had just returned from Lucas's Coffee-house, where the City Hall now stands.

20 The great Abbey of St. Thomas Court in Dublin also belonged to this Order. It was situated in Thomas Street, which s named from it, and was dedicated to St. Thomas Becket, the martyred Archbishop of Canterbury.

21 There is a Dublin in Wales and one in Canada. There is a county of Dublin in Queensland, and there are twenty-four Dublins in the United States.

22 West of Finglas, on the Ratoath Road, is Cappagh or Cappoge, once the property of the Corrigan family, and now a Home for St. Joseph's Children Hospital, Temple Street.

23 Sir Thomas Staples, who died in 1865, was the last survivor of the Irish House of Commons, in which he had represented the borough of Knocktopher in Kilkenny.

24 Like the River Poddle on the south side of Dublin, or the Swan River in Rathmines.

25 Besides the Pill or estuary near Ormond Market there was Usher's Pill near Usher's Island on the south side of the Liffey.

26 Few would expect to find a reference to the Dublin 'Liberty Boys' in such a work as Scott's *Antiquary*, and yet they are referred to in that romance in a remark of Edie Ochiltree, an old soldier of the Black Watch or 42nd Highlanders. The Liberty Boys had successfully resisted an attempt of

General Dilkes, the Commander-in-Chief of Ireland in the middle of the eighteenth century, to cover the graves of their relatives with lime in Bully's Acre Graveyard, Kilmainham.

27 They had also their separate graveyard in Dublin beside the Cabbage Garden Burying Ground in Cathedral Lane, Kevin Street; and afterwards, where the high wall and gate may still be seen, at the junction of Stephen's Green and Men-ion Row. In course of time they became merged in the general body of Dublin Protestants, and have been distinguished for their ability. The only token of their presence amongst us still is the occurrence of such surnames as Latouche, Journeaux, Tabuteau, Tibeaudo, Maturin, Ductos, Lefanu, Lefroy, Chenevix, Logier, Borough, Labatt, Labertouche, Lanauze, Le Clerc, Le Bas, Montfort, Fleury, Espinasse, Bessonett, Moulang, D'Olier, Perrin, Saurin, Boursiquot, Bosanquet, Dubedat, Boileau, Chaigneau, Blaquiere, Dufour and Crommelin. Cork, Lisburn and Portarlington had each a Huguenot colony.

28 Annesley resided as a boy in Phoenix Street with Purcell, a butcher of Beef Row, Ormond Market, and also in Jervis Street.

29 The title, which had become extinct in 1769, was revived in 1816.

30 Cowley Place was to have reached the Royal canal Bank near the 4ᵗʰ Lock, as the old maps show. It was to have been the eastern entrance to the Royal Circus. The corresponding western entrance was to have been a new street, opposite to Cowley Place, almost exactly on the spot where St. Joseph's Church now stands. This street is marked as Margaret Place, and like the actual Margaret Place (1818), N.C.R., near Russell Place, appears to have derived its name from the wife, afterwards widow, of Lord Mountjoy, Margaret, daughter of Hector Wallis of Russell Place.

31 The house now known as 65 Mountjoy Square West, was the residence of Piers Geale, Crown Solicitor, who became allied to many noble families by the marriages of his daughters. His house was called the House of Lords.

32 Called O'Connell Street from 1870 to 1885, Gerald Griffin Street 1885-6, and O'Connell Avenue since.

33 The Hospital has been transferred to Wyckham, Dundrum.

34 Some other examples of odd street names in Dublin, most of them still existing, are The Appian Way, Roper's Rest, Harmony Row, Misery Hill, Wormwood Gate (Gormund's Gate), Thundercut Alley, Cheater's (really

Chaytor's) Lane, Ship (Sheep) Street, Engine (formerly Indian) Alley, Cross Poddle, Thomas Court Bawn, Long Entry, Usher's Island, Rapparee Alley (Glover's Alley), Adam and Eve Lane, Salutation Alley, Marrowbone Lane, Elbow Lane, Fortuneteller's Lane, Brock Lane and Badger's Lane, Hoggen Green, Three Nun Alley, Minchin's Mantle (site of Kildare Street), Artichoke Road (Shelbourne Road), Faithful Place, Crooked Staff (Ardee Street), Behind Street, Golden Bridge, 'Rialto' Bridge, Cross Stick Alley, Carman's Hall and Cow Parlour.

35 Fortunately this name was discarded in time before the word New became inappropriate as in the case of New Street, New Row and Newmarket, which are all old, particularly the first.

36 Johnston designed also the castle chapel, the General Post Office and the extensions of the Viceregal Lodge.

37 Luke Gardiner, son of the Right Hon. Charles Gardiner, was born in 1745. He was member for the County of Dublin in the Irish Parliament, and was honourably distinguished as an advocate of the relaxation of the Penal Laws in an age when many otherwise patriotic Irishmen, such as Charlemont, Charles Lucas and Speaker Foster, were opposed to such relaxation. Gardiner's proposals for complete equality of the Catholics with other Irishmen were defeated. He was violently opposed by Fitzgibbon, afterwards Earl of Clare, whose father had once been a Catholic. He intended to grant an advantageous lease to the Poor Clares for their Convent in Hardwicke Street, but his premature death prevented this, and they migrated to Harold's Cross, He was created Baron Mountjoy in 1789 and Viscount Mountjoy in 1795. He was connected with a family of Lords Mountjoy and Earls of Blessington, whose title had become extinct. They were Stewarts, an Ulster family of Scottish origin, and derived their title from Mountjoy in Co. Tyrone. The word is like, but unconnected with, the old French war-cry of 'Montjoie St. Denis'. Lord Mountjoy was Colonel of the County Dublin Militia. He accompanied that regiment when it was sent to fight the Wexford insurgents and was killed at the Battle of New Ross on the 5th of June, 1798. His second wife, who was widowed by this event, was a member of a family who lived in Russell Place, in this part of Dublin, for nearly a century Lord Mountjoy was succeeded in his title and great estates by his only son Charles (from whom Great Charles Street was apparently named) who was created Earl of Blessington

in 1816, and died in 1829, when all the titles became extinct. His widow, whose maiden name was Margaret Power, a native of Tipperary, was the Countess of Blessington, whose name was so well known in the thirties and forties of the last century in London literary and fashionable circles. Charles Gardiner, Earl of Blessington and Lord Mountjoy, is said to have had an income of £30,000 a year. The Gardiner property comprised the finest streets and best houses on the north side of Dublin.

38 At a still earlier period we find the Jesuits, as in recent years, taking care of the University education of Ireland, not in St. Stephen's Green but in Back Lane. They owed this house to the generosity of Lady Kildare. She was Elizabeth daughter of Christopher Nugent, Lord Delvin, and wife of Gerald, fourteenth Earl of Kildare. In 1631 Lancelot Bulkeley, Protestant Archbishop of Dublin, made a predatory incursion on the Jesuits' University, and not only suppressed it, but transferred its property to Trinity College. The Jesuits and the Irish Catholics were persecuted together for many years after, and it must be always a consolation for Irishmen to reflect that, although some unworthy Catholics in other countries were responsible for causing the suppression of the great Society, faithful and persecuted Ireland had no feeling but sorrow and sympathy for the Jesuits.

When Pius VII restored the Jesuits, on the 7th of August, 18 by the Bull *Sollicitudine Omnium Ecclesiarum*, the celebrated Father Peter Kenny founded Clongowes wood College, in Castle Browne, County Kildare. He is said to have preferred this site, as he had spent the years of his boyhood near it, to one in the Diocese of Meath offered by Dr. Plunkett, the Bishop.

39 Rochfort, the family name of the Lords Belvedere, still exists in Rochfortbridge, County Westmeath, which was called after them, and in the Rochfort-Boyd family which has inherited much of their property in that county. But another large portion, with Belvedere House, near Belvedere Lake or Lough Ennel, belongs to the Marlay family. In a volume of Poetry published recently, a striking poem may be found commemorating the legend of the *Headless Coach of Belvedere*, still current in Westmeath.

40 For further particulars of the history of this famous Dublin school and its pupils the reader is referred to the *Belvederian*.

41 In the last quarter of the eighteenth century and the beginning of the nineteenth, there were many noble residents of streets on the north side of Dublin. Amongst them may be mentioned viscount Mountgarrett in Great Britain Street (the house is now part of the Rotunda Hospital), also Lady Alice Hume at the corner of Dominick Street, and viscount Duncannon at Nos. 204 and 205 in Lower Dominick Street, the Hon. Henry King at No. 10. 11 Sir Hercules Langrishe, 16 Lord Ely, 20 Lord Ffrench, and 41 the Earl Of Howth; in Dorset Street, Lord Dartrey in 2 Gardiner's Row, Lord Ashtown; 4, the Earl of Arran; 5 the Earl of Ross, and 6, the Earl of Carrick and afterwards Mr. Luke white; at 2 Lower Gardiner Street, Viscount Molesworth; at No. 3 Henrietta Street, the Earl of Kingston; 6, Lord Thomond; 9, Lord O'Neill; 10, the Earl of Blessington and Viscount Mountjoy; 11 the Earl of Shannon; in Marlborough Street, the Marquess of Waterford at Tyrone House; in the present No. 82 (the cathedral Presbytery), and afterwards in the present Nos. 86 and 87, viscount Avonmore; in 35 North Great George's Street, the Earl of Kenmare; in Gloucester Street, the Marquess of Downshire; at to Upper Sackville Street, the Earl of Drogheda; 12, the Earl of Glandore; at is Lord Sunderlin; at 18 the Marquess of Sligo; at 19, Lord Netterville; at 24, Viscount Pery; on the western side of the street, called Gardiner's Mall, the Earl of Leitrim lived at No. 40; at 42, Lord Gosford; at 45 (now so), Lord Clarina; 56, Lord Bangor; 7, the Earl of Belmore; and 58, Lord Cremorne. In Rutland Square, Lord Wicklow lived at No. 4; at 10, Lord Longford; 11 Lord Ormonde; 17 the Earl of Bective; 18, Lord Farnham; 24, Lord Westmeath; 31, Lord Darnley; the large house, 34, Thomas Adderley, stepfather of Lord Charlemont, and principally responsible for the education of the Volunteer Earl, who lived at No. 22; at 39, Lord Enniskillen; 41, Lord Erne, and 44 Lord Dillon. In 14, Temple Street, Lord Lismore in the house in which Charles Stewart Parnell resided from 1862 to 1867; and in 15, the Earl of Bellamont. Both of these houses are now part of St. Joseph's Children Hospital.

42 Another great Irishman, Thomas Moore, the poet, died on the same day.

43 Lennox Street takes its name also from this family. Charles Lennox, the first Duke, was a son of Charles II. The fourth Duke, a general in the army, was Lord Lieutenant from 1807 to 1813. Two years later he was present at Waterloo. It was he and his wife who gave the historic ball in Brussells

on the evening of Thursday, the 15th of June, 1815. The troops marched out of the city to the front on that night, and the battle of Les Quatre Bras took place on the next day. Two days later the greater battle was fought. Wellington came to this ball, and it is mentioned in all histories of the campaign. Our readers will remember the splendid stanzas of *Childe Harold* in which Byron commemorates the ball and the battle. It is also introduced very effectively by Thackeray into *Vanity Fair*. The fourth Duke of Richmond, whose wife gave the ball, was an honest and capable man both as soldier and administrator. He died Governor-General of Canada in 1819.

44 The road leading to Drumcondra, called Drumcondra Road, gradually came to be confounded with that district itself. Similarly, in the northern suburbs of Dublin, Ballybough Road, Glasnevin Road, Phibsborough Road and Cabra Road, originally roads leading to those localities are now considered the most important parts of the localities. All the townlands of Cabra are quite a long distance beyond the last houses of Cabra Road.

45 Ekowe Terrace is called after a place in South Africa, where the British were besieged during the Zulu War in 1879.

46 And also the Irish Parliament House, the Custom House, the King's Inns and Carlisle Bridge.

47 North County Dublin contains townlands bearing the following names: Puckstown, Tankardstown, Nutstown, Saucerstown. Kitchenstown, Folkstown, Warblestown. Rallekaystown, Buzzardstown, Hazardstown, Winnings, Folly, Bohammer. Snugborough, Salmon, Matt, Astagob, Stockhole, Tubberbunny, Coldwinters, Shallon. Stockens. Stang, Slutsend, Dellabrown, Strifeland, Swansnest, Westereve, Boggyheary. Brazil, Rahulk, Coldblow, Beau, Bridetree, Popeshall, Yellowwalls, Bay, Court, Littlepace, Coolfores, Snug, Goose Acre, Merryfalls, Balbutcher, Turnapin, Cherryhound, Miltonsfields, Crowscastle, Goddamendy, Pluckhimin, Skidoo and Skephubble. Besides these townlands the following names of places are found in Fingal: Isaac's Bower, Mabel's Well. The Cross of the Cage, Lampsoon Head. Chink Well., Mullin Intake, The Priest's Chamber (a sea cave at Donabate), Wind will. Farming's Walls, Ford of Fyne. Naptown, Juan's Well, Rux House, Sack Lane, Kit's Green, Cintra (from the Convention), Hand Park, Harp Ear, The Lord of Kerry and Lubber's Wood.

48 *Here lies an honest man without pretence, Blessed with plain reason, and with common sense; Calmly he looked on either life, and here Saw nothing to regret or there to fear; From nature's temperate feast rose satisfied, Thanked Heaven that he had lived, and that he died.* The first two lines are slightly altered from the first two lines of Pope's Epitaph on Mrs. Corbet. The last four are the last four of Pope's Epitaph on Elijah Fenton, his brother poet and collaborator in translating Homer's *Odyssey.*

49 These demesnes belong, the first to Lord Holmpatrick, the other three respectively to the families of Woods, Taylor, and Hamilton.

50 This was following a precedent set in London in the reign of Charles II when George Street, Villiers Street, Duke Street, Of Alley and Buckingham Street were named after George Villiers, Duke of Buckingham. Harry Street. Duke Street and Grafton Street, in Dublin, seem to mark a similar origin of names from Harry, Duke of Grafton, a son of Charles II, who was killed fighting at the siege of Cork in 1690. Tangier Lane, oft Grafton Street, is from Tangier in Morocco, a British possession in that King's reign. It was that sovereign who, in 1661, conferred the earldom of Drogheda on Henry Moore; and the widow of Charles, the second earl, married Wycherley, a well-known dramatist of the day. Lady Drogheda bequeathed this estate in North Dublin city to Wycherley, but her will was disputed, and the law-suit ruined the playwright, who was confined for seven years in the Fleet Prison.

51 Frederick, filth Earl of Carlisle, from whom the old bridge was named, was a poet, and a relative and guardian of Byron, who at first satirized him, but afterwards expressed regret.

52 A design of theirs, never executed, was to make a new street from York Street to St. Patrick's Cathedral.

53 Denis Florence McCarthy was born in 1817 in a house which is now a part of Messrs. Clery's. Shelley stayed for some time at 7 Lower, and De Quincey at 18 Upper Sackville Street.

54 Two other statues in this part of Dublin are from the chisel of Farrell: that of William Smith O'Brien, the Young Ireland leader, in O'Connell Street, unveiled in 1870 ; and that of Sir Alexander MacDonnell in the lawn of the Education Office, unveiled 14th August, 1878. MacDonnell had been Resident Commissioner of National Education from 1839 to 1871. He had a very distinguished academic career at Oxford, winning

four University prizes, Latin and English, verse and essay, a feat only once before accomplished.

55 There was a menagerie in the eighteenth century in the space not built upon until the beginning of the following century, between this lane and Earl Street. A large elephant is said to have been burnt here in an accidental fire. It was not customary a hundred and seventy years ago to bestow names on many lanes in Dublin, and the maps of that time merely mark the name Stable Lane on a great many lanes which now bear particular names, amongst others Cathedral Street, Nelson Lane (Earl Place) and Thomas's Lane in this district. Gregg's Lane became Findlater Place in 1881.

56 Dr. Joyces's Child's History of Ireland, p. 111.

57 Westmoreland Row, near Fitzgibbon Street, in Directories 1795-1839, seems to have disappeared.

58 Edmond O'Donovan was born at 49, now 55, Bayview Avenue, on the 13th. of September, 1844. He lived afterwards at 39 North Strand.

59 Also the name of a town in Monaghan. There are many other single-word names of streets in Dublin, such as Dolphinsbarn (1396), Grangegorman, Broadstone, Mullinahack, Mountbrown, Warren-mount, Portobello, Gibraltar, Rowserstown, Mockenstown, Phibs-borough, Stonybatter, Coombe, Pigtown, Cadslough, Blackpits, Newmarket, Rehoboth, Tripoli, Pimlico, Spitalfields, Lotts, Mespil, Nickleby, and Uxbridge.

60 The building of the Custom House, with quays and docks, is said to have cost half a million of money.

61 Dickens has been honoured in Dublin by the name of Pickwick Place, off Great Strand Street, built the year after the appearance (1837) of *Pickwick;* and by the name of Nickleby built in 1840, a year after that book was published. Nickleby, off Mecklenburgh Street, was absorbed by the Penitentiary in 1896. Pickwick Place exists still-but has borne no name-plate for many years. It must originally have been not unlike some of the London inns in the book.

62 The Offices of the Board, for the first three years of its existence, 1832-5, were in Mornington House, 24 Upper Merrion Street, the birthplace of the Duke of Wellington, now the office of the Land Commission.

63 William Beresford, the victor of Albuera in the Peninsular War, who was created Field Marshal and Viscount, was a member of this family. Another, whose fame is of a different sort, was John Claudius Beresford,

whose Riding School, near the Talbot Street side of the premises, is said to have been a place of torture by flogging for suspected persons in 1798. He resided in the large house 9 Upper Buckingham Street, afterwards St. Joseph's Children's Hospital. But the most notable and powerful member of the family was the Commissioner of Revenue, already mentioned, who caused the new Custom House to be built in this neighbourhood.

64 According to Fitzpatrick, but a correspondent of the *Irish Builder,* June, 1891, asserts that he was born in Mulberry Lodge, Philipsburgh Lane (this is the house now known as 6 Philipsburgh Avenue), and that he lived at the present No. 67 Talbot Street.

65 Amongst other distinguished men horn on the north side of Dublin, may be mentioned John O'Keeffe, the dramatist, born in Abbey Street. William Mossop, the medallist, Dion Boucicault, the dramatist, in North Earl Street, and Joseph Sheridan Lefanu, the novelist, at 52 Lower Dominick Street (See Rev. Br. W. A. Swan's *Our Civic Highways)*.

66 Old Strandville Avenue runs from Clontarf Railway Station to the sea, which it meets at Brookside, where the Holly Brook flows into the Bay.

67 His family also founded the town of Stratford-on-Slaney in Wicklow, in which county and those of Kildare and Carlow, the family estates lay.

68 Lord Aldborough built another great house in London and died in 1801. The last Earl of Aldborough died at Alicante in Spain in 1875 when the title became extinct. He had made several attempts to construct flying machines.

69 The name Custom House Quay had been given for many years previously to the quay where the Old Custom House stood from 1621 to 1791 beside Essex Bridge. This quay received in 1817 two years after Waterloo, its present name of Wellington Quay. Wellington Bridge, called the Metal Bridge, and the Wellington Obelisk in the Phoenix Park date from the same time, being recognitions of Wellington's fame in his native city.

70 The Monument, the tallest isolated column in the world, erected by Wren to commemorate the Great Fire of London, stands on Fish Street Hill.

71 Portions of the North Circular Road are, at its western extremity, Conyngham Road and Infirmary Road; and, at its eastern, Portland Row, Seville Place and Guild Street.

72 William Carleton, the Ulster novelist, lived at No. 4 Whitworth Row. An unpublished novel of his exists in MS., entitled *Anne Cosgrave.*

73 Princess Charlotte, only child of George IV, was married in 1816 to Prince
    Leopold of Coburg. She died in 1817, and he afterwards became Leopold I,
    King of the Belgians. Coburgh Gardens had been previously the grounds
    of the Earl of Clonmell's town-house in Harcourt Street.

74 It is more likely that work began on this Church in 1858 and was finished
    after 1859.

75 The Church of St. Joseph, on Church Road, was built a few years ago to
    serve this rapidly-growing district.

76 This map, of which a later edition was produced showing the Royal
    Canal, represents as to be reclaimed all the space still covered by the
    sea between the East Wall and Clontarf Strand Road, westward of a line
    drawn from the Wharf to a point opposite to Clontarf. That line was
    to have been a new coast road called 'Island Key', a continuation of the
    'East Key' (part of the East Wall), It was to have crossed each end of
    Clontarf Island, leaving the centre of the Island stilt separated from the
    mainland by a lake or small portion of the sea. There were to have been
    three other roads, parallel to this new coast road, connecting the East
    Wall with Clontarf Road, and all three traversing the space where the
    tide still ebbs and flows, (1) Island Road, a continuation of the East Road;
    (2) Market Road, a continuation of Church Road, And (3) Hollybrook
    Road, a continuation of the West Road, and intended no doubt, to reach
    Clontarf Strand in the district of Hollybrook.

    Within the last twenty years a real Hollybrook Road has been made
    in that part of Clontarf, not on land reclaimed from the sea, however,
    but running off the coast road. Besides all these extensive changes there
    was to be a 'New Canall', running close by the East Wall, and obviously
    representing the course of the Tolka from its mouth at Annesley Bridge
    to a point beyond the North Wall Extension, an item which must always
    be taken into account in projects of reclamation here. The coming of the
    Great Northern Railway has changed the conditions of the reclamation,
    yet the latter seems to be actually following the exact plan of that 'New
    Canall' of 1717.

77 In Sheriff Street was situated the Prison (Castle Forbes) where the French
    prisoners of war were confined, who were captured in the great War
    beginning with the Revolution and ending in the fall of Napoleon.

78 There is a place of nearly the same name in the County of Meath.

79 Dame Gate was the eastern extremity of Dublin then, being next to the Church of Our Lady del Dam, from which Dame Street takes its name.

80 The next Archbishop, sent from England, was George Browne, the first to support Henry VII in his schism from Rome.

81 Readers of Lever's *Maurice Tiernay* will remember that the hero, born in France of Irish extraction, takes part in the temporary success and ultimate defeat of the French in Ireland in 1798. In the course of the story he takes up his residence with one Tiernay a farmer near Baldoyle. Lever evidently studied that district from Moatfield.

82 On the east of Coolock village, 'Shilling Glass' is marked on old maps. Perhaps it was the sign of an inn.

83 It is known positively that he was baptized at St. John's Church, Fishamble Street, Dublin, on the 3rd of July, 1746. The precise day of his birth does not seem to be known. His father, James Grattan, Recorder of Dublin, and Member of Parliament for the City, was a member of the Conservative party of that day. Disapproving of what he considered Henry's advanced national views he took care that the latter should not inherit Belcamp, which had been a long time in the Grattan family. Miss Olivia Whitmore, cousin of Henry Grattan, was married to Arthur Guinness of Beaumont, great grandfather of Lords Ardilaun and Iveagh.

84 In 1776 the Declaration of Independence had been issued. In 1777 the British commander Burgoyne had surrendered at Saratoga to the Americans, and in 1778, the year the tower was erected here. France espoused the now thriving cause of the Americans, sending some of her Irish Brigade to the last war they ever fought in. Spain and Holland were soon to follow France's example, and the war was to drag on for four more weary years until, after the surrender of Cornwallis at Yorktown, England was to acknowledge American Independence. Yet under all these circumstances the Government allowed Sir Edward Newenham to erect with impunity the Washington tower at Belcamp. Perhaps the authorities were deterred from interfering by the sympathy felt for the Americans by the then powerful Irish Volunteers.

85 She is one of the trinity of little known saints to whom parishes in the City of Dublin were dedicated the other two being St. Audoen or Ouen, Bishop of Rouen, who also died in 683, having his feast on the 24th of August, and St. Michan, whose feast is the following day, the 25th of August, a Scandinavian bishop of whom little is known.

86 The Talbots of Carton, Maynooth, were cousins of the Malahide Talbots. Two younger Sons of Sir William Talbot, Bart., of Carton, were amongst the most famous Irishmen of the seventeenth century. One was Peter Talbot who entered the Society of Jesus in his youth and remained in it many years. Having left it he became a secular priest, and was in 1669 appointed by the Pope, Archbishop of Dublin. He died in prison in 1680 being accused in connection with the Irish branch of Titus Oates's Plot. Had he survived a few months longer he would have been martyred along with his fellow-prisoner the Blessed Oliver Plunket. The Archbishop's brother was Richard Talbot, created Earl of Tyrconnel, a faithful adherent of Charles II and James II. In the reign of the latter he was Lord Lieutenant of Ireland, being the last Catholic for more than two centuries who held that position. He was in possession at one time of an estate in the southern part of the County Dublin, Terenure, now the Carmelite College. Tyrconnell fought for James in the war and died in Limerick during the siege. His widow founded the Convent of Poor Clares in North King Street, already referred to.

87 See The Churches of Fingal by Archdeacon Walsh.

88 There is another Clontarf, named after this, on the harbour of Sydney, Australia. There are two places called Clontarf in the United States—one in Minnesota and one in Wisconsin; and there is a third in Canada.

89 There are Martello Towers at Balbriggan, Skerries, Shenick Island, Loughshinny, Rush, Portrane (two), Robertswall, Carrick Hill, Ireland's Eye, Howth, and also at Sandymount, Williamstown, Seapoint, Dun Laoghaire, Sandycove, Bullock, Dalkey Island, Killiney, Shanganagh and Bray.

90 Howth in Texas is called after this hill.

91 Readers of the marvellous analytical stories of Edgar Poe will remember how, in one of them, an investigator identifies the 'Bishop's Hostel' of the cryptogram with Bessop's Castle, which he discovers to be a wild cliff, containing the Devil's Seat, on the coast of Sullivan's Island, South Carolina.